SECRET
BALI

Narina Exelby
& Mark Eveleigh

JONGLEZ PUBLISHING
travel guides

Narina Exelby is a freelance writer and editor who swapped stability in Cape Town and 15 years in the international magazine industry for freedom and life on the road. Her default setting has always been to seek out quiet spaces, which is one of the reasons Narina's base for the past few years has been the far west coast of Bali, four hours away from the crowds. She travels frequently – mostly around South East Asia, Southern Africa and Europe – and when she leaves her treehouse sanctuary for a city, she revels in the chance to drink good wine and indulge in cheese ... and is often surprised by the delight she finds in the rhythm of big city life.

Six nerve-wracking hours dangling from a frayed cable in a Venezuelan cable-car sent Mark Eveleigh into free-fall on a career as travel writer, specialising in adventure. He taught himself Indonesian in preparation for an expedition he led into Central Borneo's "valley of the spirit world" (which became the subject for his first book, *Fever Trees of Borneo*). Mark fell in love with Bali when he spent a year living with a Balinese family in 2003 and for more than five years now his writing base has been in the island's "wild west". Although he's covered assignments in more than 100 Indonesian islands (for BBC, CNN, Esquire, National Geographic Traveller and others), Mark still describes the remoter parts of Bali as "a forgotten paradise".

Some people might be surprised to hear that there are any secrets left in Bali. Traditionally celebrated as one of the world's most beautiful places, Bali has more often been described in recent years as "spoiled" and "overcrowded". This book is a homage to an island paradise that still bewitches those who take the time to explore it. More than that, it is a tribute to the Balinese people – one of the richest and most hospitable cultures in the world. Some of the places in this book are located in parts of the island that few visitors ever see; others lie like dropped gems, right beside the well-trodden tourist trail. Even dedicated connoisseurs of Bali are sure to find some treasures among these pages.

Descriptions of certain locations are accompanied by thematic sections highlighting cultural details or anecdotes as an aid to understanding one of the world's most mysteriously complex islands.

Note that when visiting a home or workshop there is usually no entry fee, but donations would be gratefully accepted. Some museums and studios do charge a minimal entry fee; those that charge a fee of Rp75,000 or higher have been noted on the relevant pages.

Comments on this guidebook and its contents, as well as information on deserving 'secret spots' we may not have mentioned, are more than welcome and will enrich future editions.

Don't hesitate to contact us:
E-mail: info@jonglezpublishing.com
Jonglez Publishing, 25 rue du Maréchal Foch
78000 Versailles, France

Taman National Park
Java Island
Prapat Agung Peninsula
BALI SEA
Gilimanuk
Seriri
Banyuwangi
West Bali National Park
WEST BALI
Pupua
Negara
Medewi
B
Kali Setail
Bali Strait
p. 46
Jl-227
T
Alas Purwo National Park
N
0
20 km
40 km

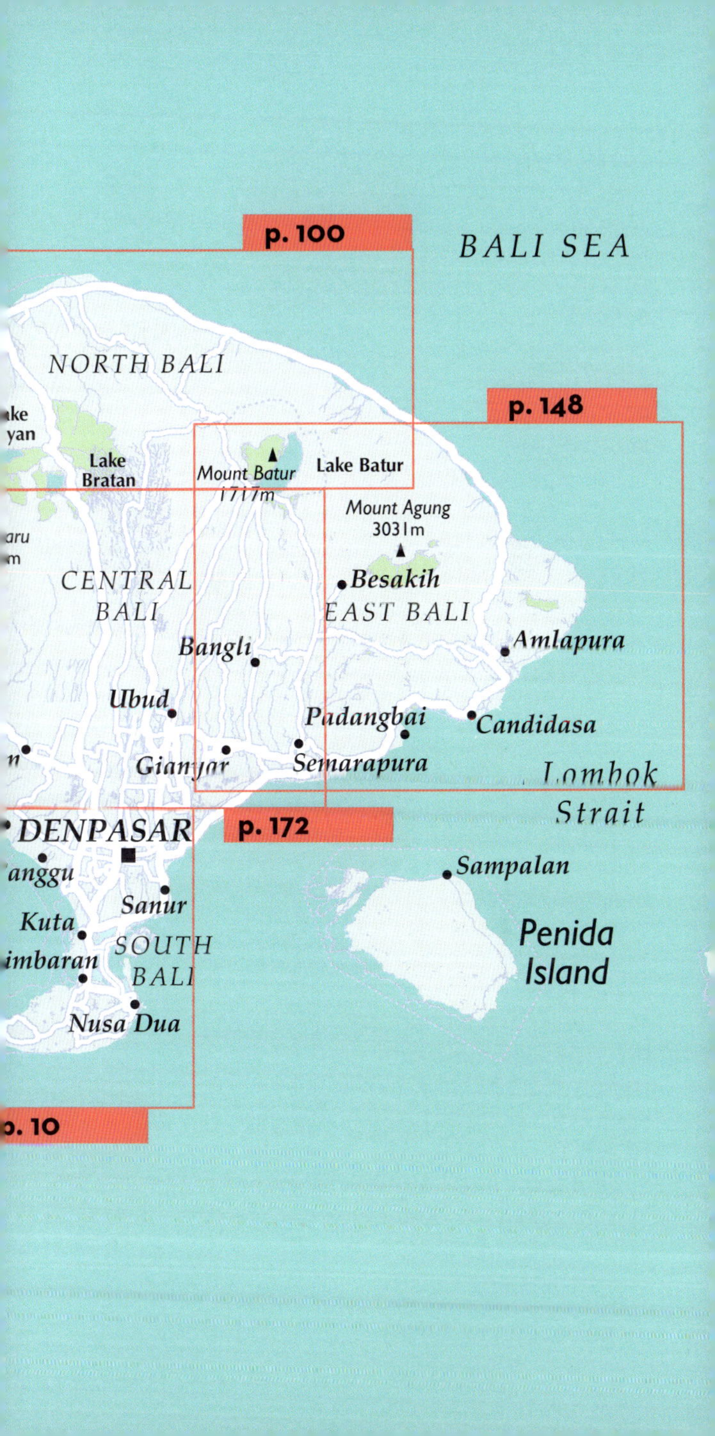

p. 100
BALI SEA
NORTH BALI
p. 148
Lake Bratan
Mount Batur 1717m
Lake Batur
Mount Agung 3031m
CENTRAL BALI
Besakih
EAST BALI
Bangli
Amlapura
Ubud
Padangbai
Candidasa
Gianyar
Semarapura
Lombok Strait
DENPASAR
p. 172
Sanur
Kuta
SOUTH BALI
Nusa Dua
Sampalan
Penida Island

CONTENTS

South Bali

West Bali

North Bali

CONTENTS

East Bali

Central Bali

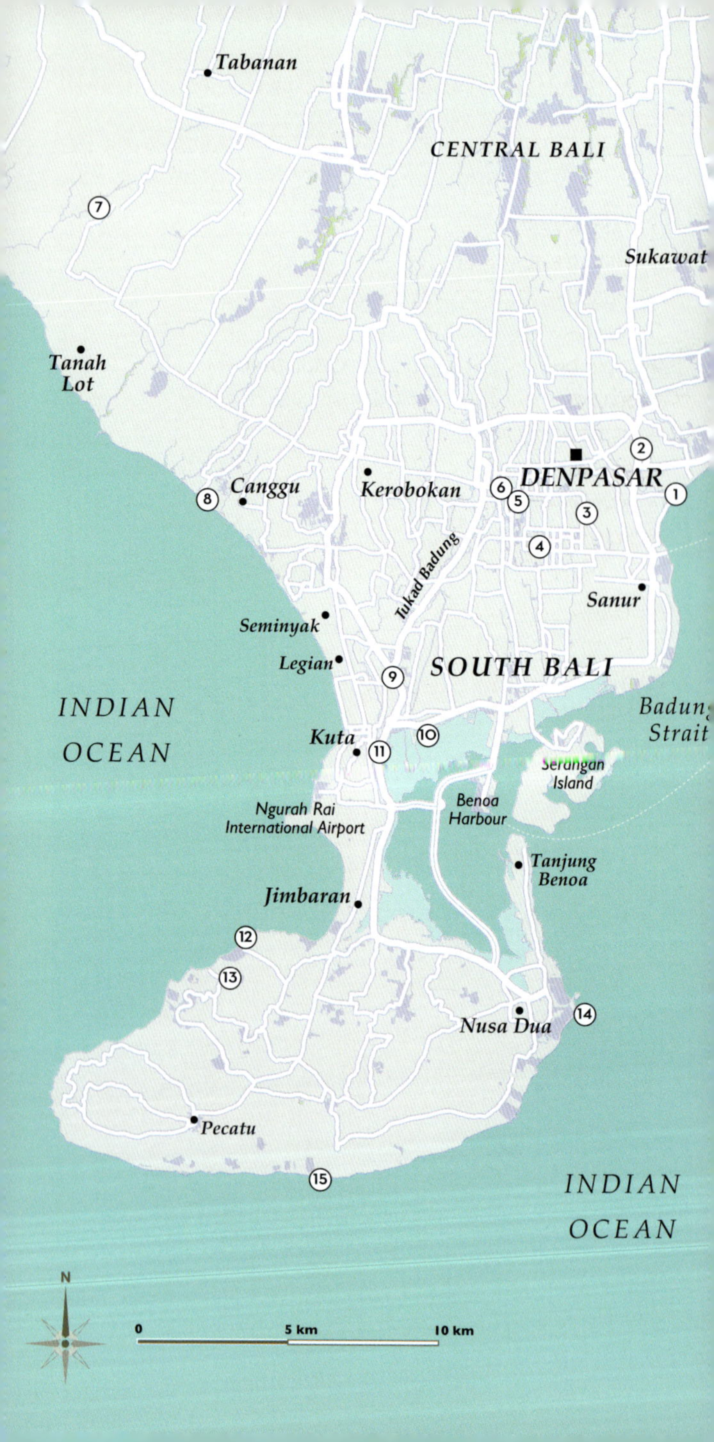
Tabanan
CENTRAL BALI
7
Sukawat
Tanah Lot
2
DENPASAR
1
Canggu
Kerobokan
8
6
5
3
4
Tukad Badung
Sanur
Seminyak
Legian
SOUTH BALI
9
INDIAN OCEAN
Badung Strait
Kuta
10
11
Serangan Island
Ngurah Rai International Airport
Benoa Harbour
Tanjung Benoa
Jimbaran
12
13
14
Nusa Dua
Pecatu
15
INDIAN OCEAN
N
0
5 km
10 km

South Bali

TAMAN FESTIVAL

①

An abandoned amusement park: Bali's spookiest landmark?

Jalan Padang Galak no. 3, Kesiman, Denpasar
Open daily

At one moment spine-chillingly haunting, the next charmingly evocative of *Jungle Book* romance, this place conjures up many images. This amusement park, abandoned in the 1990s, is fast being re-colonised by rioting vegetation, and as vines and creepers crawl over the carved façades, it is taking on a charm reminiscent of an entire complex of lost jungle temples. The fact that some stunning graffiti portraits leer out from hidden corners, adding a splash of colour and another hint of otherworldliness, makes it all the more enchanting. Squirrels skip across crumbling stonework, lizards rustle in the undergrowth, and bats flit through the shadows of desolate theatres.

The roots of an ancient banyan tree (a witness to times long before the park was even conceived of) crawl poignantly across a sculpted rainforest mural above what was once the Turbo Theatre. Peering through the pillars from the back of the lobby is a wonderful spray-painted graffiti portrait of an Aztec warrior. The cross-cultural combination makes the spot even

more intriguing ... and a cautious exploration of the pitch-black depths of the theatre itself must be one of Bali's spookiest experiences.

It is likely that the 20 or so haunting buildings in Taman Festival now offer a more invigorating visitor experience than they might have done when they were opened in 1997. The park had the world's first inverted rollercoaster, a man-made volcano, a whole extravaganza of 3D experiences and laser shows, Bali's biggest swimming pool, and crocodiles (although not in the same pool).

But Taman Festival was (quite literally) a flash in the pan.

"It was just too expensive," a security guard at the site shrugs. "Admission was Rp75,000 at a time when you could get a local meal for Rp2,000."

Rumours abound as to what actually happened. The most likely story relates to the US$5 million worth of laser equipment that was designed to make a lightshow of the night sky. Ironically, it was on Friday the 13th (in March 1998) that freak lightning scored a direct hit on the laser. The insurance money was never forthcoming and doors closed finally in 2000. Almost two decades later it is said that disputes are still ongoing about ownership of the eight-hectare plot, and these days you stand a good chance of having the deserted park to yourself.

The wildest tales concern the crocs that are said to still roam wild around the park. Some say they were fed by locals – and some very unlikely reports even suggest that they fed on locals. Security guards at the sight told us that they were sent to a reptile park near Ubud ... but actually they are now at the Bali Wildlife Rescue Centre in Tabanan (see page 224).

MEKAR BHUANA CENTRE

②

Where new life is breathed into Bali's history of music and dance

Jalan Gandapura 3 no. 501X, Kertalangu, Denpasar
081 999 191 104
balimusicanddance.com
Visits by appointment. Sunday family music sessions begin around 10am; those interested in attending should contact the centre beforehand.
Entry by donation

To an untrained ear the music of Bali could sound, well, simply like music. But *gamelan*, which is the name given to the large ensemble of mostly percussion instruments that create the music, is recognised as one

of the world's most sophisticated musical traditions. There are more than 45 different types of *gamelan* around Bali, and the Mekar Bhuana Centre in Denpasar is the only place on the island where such a great collection of the island's musical heritage has been gathered, appreciated, researched and promoted.

As with so much of Bali's culture, the music and dance traditions of the island are incredibly complex. Someone who knows *gamelan* will be able to listen to a piece of music and identify which part of the island it originates from, the instruments that are played, the purpose of the music, and what dance would accompany it. Some of the music and dance styles are becoming increasingly rare, to the point of near extinction. Mekar Bhuana is dedicated to documenting, recording and reconstructing these traditions.

"It's easy for people to think that the musical traditions of Bali are thriving because of all of the ceremonies that happen regularly," says ethnomusicologist Vaughan Hatch, co-founder of Mekar Bhuana Centre. "But when you begin to look at the details of the music, that's what's getting lost. That's what we want to preserve."

But don't visit the centre expecting to find a museum. At Mekar Bhuana, music and dance is kept alive; it is learned, performed and recreated in workshops and private lessons that cater to all levels of ability. The workshops and lessons for foreigners help to fund the centre's research and recording, and Mekar Bhuana puts a lot of effort into encouraging young Balinese in particular to place value on and take pride in their musical traditions.

The centre has a fascinating collection of unique *gamelan* instruments. "One of our rare instruments is the four-tubed *angklung kocok*, which is a bamboo rattle. While there are still three-tubed versions in some villages, we are yet to find a village that has a four-tubed version," explains Vaughan. "The *angklung kocok* we have was reconstructed from a photo taken in the 1930s by Canadian musicologist Colin McPhee. This instrument is part of one of our full *angklung* sets, which has 27 instruments in total."

Music has always been an integral part of village life in Bali, and in keeping with this, on most Sundays the centre hosts a casual family gathering where music – including sometimes the *angklung kocok* – is played. Visitors are welcome to attend.

A House in Bali, written by musicologist and composer Colin McPhee in 1946, is a beautifully evocative novel that captures both life in Bali and the spirit of music on the island. McPhee set up home and lived in Bali for almost a decade, during which he sought out and documented as much music as he could. *A House in Bali* is a lovely introduction to life on the island and well worth a read for those interested in Bali's art and music.

MUSEUM OF FINGERPRINT PAINTING

③

A museum where "hand-made" takes on a new meaning

Jalan Hayam Wuruk no. 175, Denpasar
0361 235 115
Monday–Saturday 8am–4pm
Entry by donation

The phrase "finger painting" might conjure images of paint that's been pushed and dragged around a canvas, sometimes with care but most often in a rush of sheer delight. Take one quick look around the Museum Lukisan Sidik Jari – the Museum of Fingerprint Painting – and you'll quickly realise that there's a world of difference between "finger painting" and "fingerprint painting".

The creator of the works in this museum is the well-known Balinese artist Ngurah Gede Pemecutan, who started to paint with a brush in 1954. He wasn't very satisfied with the work he was producing so he began to experiment, and by 1967 he had found his niche – creating beautiful works of art by applying paint only with the tips of his fingers. The result: intricate works of art that when viewed close up are a mesmerising series of dots, but when seen from a few steps back, the viewer's eyes trick the brain into seeing a complete image.

This style of painting, called pointillism, is usually done with brushes, and emerged from Impressionism in the late 1880s. It gained popularity in Europe but in Bali this form of art was virtually unheard of, and Ngurah Gede Pemecutan taught himself his own version of the style, earning himself the nickname "Sidik Jari Painter", or Fingerprint Painter.

Most of the paintings in the museum depict Balinese life: traditional dancers, portraits of women wearing *kubaya* (the lace shirt worn with sarong and sash), temple ceremonies. There is also Ngurah Gede Pemecutan's first fingerprint painting, which is of a Baris dancer.

Probably the largest painting in the museum is one that depicts the 1906 Pemecutan War, the battle between the Kingdon of Badung and the Dutch – he will never sell this piece, the artist has stated, because it is a memoir of his family who died in the *puputan* (see pages 29 and 165).

BUNG KARNO MUSEUM

4

Museum dedicated to Indonesia's first president

Jalan Raya Puputan no. 80, Dangin Puri Klod, Denpasar
0813 8450 0092
Tuesday–Sunday 10am–5pm

Indonesia's first president, in office from 1945 to 1967, was a charismatic man named Sukarno. Born in Surabaya to a Javanese father and a Balinese Hindu mother, he was initially named Kusnasosro, but his parents renamed him Sukarno – a more auspicious name, it was hoped – after he recovered from a series of childhood illnesses. Like many Javanese people, he had only one name. During Indonesia's struggle for independence Sukarno became known as Bung ("brother" or "comrade") Karno – the Bung Karno Museum is a tribute to the man credited with leading the 17,000-island nation to liberation. At the front of the building is an inscription of the Pancasila, Sukarno's five-point principles of an independent Indonesia.

The museum contains one of Sukarno's cars (a black Mercedes), a 1,400-book library, and furniture that belonged to him, as well as copies of his speeches and writings (he was known as a brilliant orator), a bicycle, his bed, sets of chairs, personal belongings, and scores of paintings. Look out for the painting of Nyi Roro Kidul, mythical queen of the Southern Sea, which is very similar to the painting at the shrine dedicated to the queen at the Grand Inna Bali Beach Hotel (see page 43).

Sukarno mastered Javanese, Sundanese, Balinese and modern Indonesian – which he did much to create. He also spoke Dutch, German, French, English and Japanese. While revered for leading the struggle for independence, Sukarno was never very popular in Bali, where people considered him responsible for a series of natural disasters (including a rat infestation and an eruption of Mount Agung) that befell the island during his presidency. The gods were not happy, the Balinese say.

Incidentally, the Bung Karno Museum was opened in 2015 by Megawati Soekarno Putri, the daughter of Sukarno and fifth president of Indonesia.

Sukarno's name is also spelled Soekarno. In school he was told to use the Dutch spelling – "oe", not "u". When signing his name the old habit stuck – but Sukarno insisted others spell his name with a "u". Official presidential decrees printed his name with the Dutch spelling, however, as per his signature, and Jakarta's Soekarno-Hatta International Airport carries the Dutch spelling. Mohammad Hatta, Indonesia's first vice-president, was Sukarno's long-term friend and comrade-in-arms.

COIN DISPLAY IN THE BULELENG BUILDING ⑤

Where coins have a lot more than monetary value

Bali Museum
Jalan Mayor Wisnu no. 1, Denpasar
Saturday – Thursday 8:30am–4pm; Friday 8:30am–12.30pm; closed on official holidays

The smallest of all of the buildings in the Bali Museum complex is the Buleleng Building, a pavilion that's often overlooked by visitors, but one that contains fascinating insight into the role of Chinese coins in Balinese culture. Unusually well documented for a museum display in Bali (and with English translations), the exhibitions in the Buleleng Building outline the history of Chinese coins on the island, which were official currency here from the 14th century until the 1950s, and which became integral to Hindu ceremonies.

Called *uang kepeng* in Indonesian and *pis bolong* in Balinese, the history of these coins in Bali is said to date back more than 2,000 years. In an interview with the *Jakarta Post*, coin collector and archaeology lecturer I Dewa Nyoman Putra Harthawan mentions a copper Chinese coin in his collection, found in Bali, that dates back to 175 BC. "The coin is known as a *ban liang*, or half liang," he is quoted as saying. "We have found many coins from an era 2,000 years ago. We have had intensive contact with China for more than two millennia."

Over time the coins became as integral to Hindu culture as they were to trade; popular games involving the coins were devised and, more importantly, the coins became central to offerings and ceremonies. If the *Purana* – sacred scripts – of the Pura Dalem Balingkan temple are accurate, then it's likely that the use of *kepeng* in ceremonies can be traced back to the 12th century, to the marriage of king Raja Sri Haji Jayapangus and Kang Ching Wei, the daughter of a Chinese merchant (see page 144). After the wedding ceremony the merchant gave two Chinese coins to his daughter, and the king declared that *kepeng* be used in religious ceremonies across the island in the future.

The coin display covers the entire Buleleng Building, so named because the king who financed the construction of this particular building in the early 1900s ruled over Buleleng, north Bali, and architecturally it represents the style of the temple pagodas in that area. It was one of the initial three buildings in the museum complex, which opened officially in 1932. In 1969 more land and buildings were added and the museum more than doubled in size.

The magical powers of Chinese coins

Some coins, it is still believed, hold magical powers. It's not clear when (likely between the 15th and 17th centuries, says I Dewa Nyoman Putra Harthawan), but coins began to emerge that had become "Balinised": the Chinese writing remained on one side while on the other, there were characters or images sacred in Bali, called *rerajahan*. These coins are believed to contain supernatural powers that correlate to the *rerajahan*. For example, if someone holds a *pis jaran* – a coin with a horse image – they will win a race, so long as they trust in the coin's powers.

BALINESE CALENDAR AT THE BALI MUSEUM

⑥

Marking time on the Islands of the Gods

Bali Museum
Jalan Mayor Wisnu no. 1, Dangin Puri, Denpasar
Saturday–Thursday 8:30am–4pm; Friday 8:30am–12:30pm; closed on official holidays

Stored in a cabinet in the East Building of the Bali Museum is an intriguing, intricate wooden carving displayed alongside a piece of

fabric that's been divided into elaborately painted boxes. Next to the rectangular carving – which also depicts boxes, as well as crosses and dots of different colours – is the label "Balinese calendar". It's a very rudimentary explanation of the incredibly complex system defining Bali as the culturally rich place that it is.

The fabric is a *palelintangan*, an astrological calendar that represents a Balinese month (showing the gods and symbolic forms that govern each day), while the carving is a *tika*, which acts as a visual guide to the Pawukon calendar ... and for these to make any sense, you need to understand the basics of Balinese Hindu time.

The basics of Balinese Hindu time

Time in Bali is defined by three calendars: the Gregorian calendar (introduced by the Dutch and observed for business and administrative affairs), the 210-day Pawukon calendar (used to set religious and ceremonial events) and the 12-month Saka calendar (the lunar calendar). The Pawukon and Saka calendars are not synchronised and are both still very much observed. There are very careful formulas and calculations that determine how the Pawukon calendar indicates religious events, and the process is mind-boggling. It's based more or less on the following principle: the Pawukon calendar is comprised of six 35-day months, and within it there are 10 different concurrent weeks, or cycles, each of which contains one to 10 days. Each day of each cycle has its own Sanskrit name, not a number. Of these 10 cycles, there are three that are considered more important than the others: the three-day cycle (called *Triwara*, which is used to determine market days), the five-day cycle (called *Pancawara*) and the seven-day cycle (called *Saptawara*). Auspicious days and ceremonial days are determined by "coincidence days" – for example, when the third day of the third cycle coincides with the fifth day of the fifth cycle. This happens every 15 days and, because evil spirits are particularly active on this day, more elaborate offerings are prepared.

It's through coincidences like this that almost every ceremonial day is determined – except Nyepi (see page 24), which is determined by Saka, the lunar calendar. In the Saka calendar, which originated in India, there are 12 months of 30 days; each month begins the day after the new moon. Nyepi marks the beginning of the new lunar year and is traditionally a day of silence and meditation across Bali. Nyepi usually falls during March, and around this time you're likely to see posters around Bali commemorating a year from the past – for example, celebrating 1942 when it's actually 2020. This is because years on the Saka calendar are numbered from the date that a Saka tribe came into power in south India, which was 78 AD.

The carnival before Nyepi, Bali's silent day

The beaches are deserted. The streets are dead. The habitual din of whining motorbikes has, for once, ceased to convert Sunset Road into a two-wheel drag-race. The beaches and waves are left to the turtles and even at Ngurah Rai International Airport the airplanes stand abandoned; no planes arrive, not one leaves. The tropical breeze is no longer laden with the scent of smoking satays or the gentle waft of offered incense, and in the Muslim enclaves the prayer call no longer wails out from the minarets. Sometimes it seems that even the birds have stopped singing to listen to the sound of silence. For 24 hours each year, after extensive purification ceremonies, Bali turns into a ghost island. Although many people avoid visiting at this time, being on the island for Nyepi (Bali's "silent day") is an experience they'll never forget.

On this day, which marks the beginning of the new year according to the lunar Saka calendar (see page 22), the legendary 'Island of the Gods' is believed to be overrun by demons. It is forbidden to travel, work, cook with fire, make noise or even have lights on in your house. The silence seems all the more profound because of the sheer din and clamour of the processions of the previous evening. On the eve of Nyepi, every village on the island celebrates a parade of Ogoh-Ogoh effigies (see pages 200 and 226).

In what must be one of the world's most bizarre street carnivals, giant figures – most sporting sagging breasts, lolling tongues and leering eyes – are carried through the streets. They cavort and pirouette in a hideous dance that is designed to disorientate the demons and spirits that are trying to follow them. It is believed that the evil beings that haunt the underworld find all this clamour to be so irresistible that they flock to the island. But it is all a trick, because at midnight the effigies are destroyed (with a few exceptions in recent years) and the revellers head into their silent houses. For 24 hours the demons swoop over the island, utterly confused and slowly coming to the conclusion that nobody lives on the island at all. From dawn on Nyepi day to dawn the following morning nobody shows themselves (or shines a light or reveals their presence with cooking smoke), and finally the demons leave the island in peace, convinced that they can do no mischief in a land that has apparently been totally deserted by humans.

The prohibitions surrounding Nyepi are strictly enforced. In case you're curious as to what happens if you break the rules and wander out to explore the deserted streets: you run the risk of seriously displeasing the entire (normally hospitable) island population; of being evicted from the island in disgrace; and of having to foot the bill for what could be an extremely expensive purification ceremony to undo the harm you've done.

Most resorts function more or less as normal (albeit with a skeleton staff), and you can move around as long as you stay on the premises, but if you're staying in a villa you'll have to stay inside and refrain from making any noise that can be heard outside. It is an intensely peaceful experience to have an enforced day of utter laziness, and one of the highlights as the silent dusk starts to fall is the incredible dome of stars that hovers over an island that is almost totally free from light pollution.

PEJATEN VILLAGE

⑦

One of the little-known gems of southern Bali

Banjar Pangkung, Pejaten, Kediri, Tabanan
Monday–Saturday 7am–noon
Closed for ceremony days
Free, donations gratefully accepted

Pak Dedi is one of the "terracotta warriors" of Pejatan village. He rises at dawn to start work with his family in what is one of the most fascinating industrial villages in Bali. Pak Dedi and his family are part of a pottery and ceramics tradition that stretches back generations, and he (along with his daughter, Dewi, and sons, Doni and Dani) can produce about 1,000 handmade terracotta bricks in a morning's work.

Pejaten village is one of the little-known gems of southern Bali – a village that seems to exist unaffected by the tourist invasion that preoccupies most of the region. Despite being just 5 km from the tourist attraction of Tanah Lot Temple, few people pass through Pejaten and only rarely does anyone take the time to stop. Even if you just drive slowly through the lanes of the village, you'll be astounded to see great expanses of handmade tiles and bricks laid out to dry in the sun.

Although there were no "untouchables" in Balinese Hinduism, pottery was traditionally considered "unclean" work, and so pottery centres like this used to be considered communities of outcasts. There are a couple of small showrooms showing traditional ceramics (mostly household cooking and storage vessels, but occasionally also ceremonial objects for temples), but these days, however, most of the villagers are employed in making beautiful handmade bricks and tiles.

Clay was traditionally collected from the nearby riverbed, but as sources are now running low, it is often trucked in from farther afield. The bricks are made in heavy presses that are repeatedly swung down with great effort by the operator. During breaks for a cigarette or coffee, Pak Dedi also takes a moment to relax by crooning along to the portable karaoke machine (his pride and joy), which stands next to his workstation.

The bricks are fired in two-storey kilns that are fuelled with coconut husks, and if you turn up on any working day, you can watch production at any one of the little family-run factories along the road. Pak Dedi or one of his co-workers would be happy to let you try your hand at creating a few bricks – it's heavier work than you'd imagine and you'll instantly appreciate how they get their muscular forearms. If you ask nicely, they might even let you try a tune on their karaoke machine.

BALE PUPUTAN

8

A memorial for Balinese heroes in the heart of hipster Canggu

Tugu Hotel, Jalan Pantai Batu Bolong, Canggu, Badung
0361 473 1701
Daily 8am–5pm

The busy hipster hangout of Batu Bolong Beach is the last place you might expect to learn about one of the most important periods of Balinese history. Just 100 metres from the beach-break that is known to local surfers as Old Man's, you'll find one of the most fascinating little museums on the entire island.

The Bale Puputan museum is dedicated to the Balinese heroes who died in the "Puputan Wars" of Badung (1906) and Klungkung (1908). The building is part of the luxuriously evocative Hotel Tugu Bali, but if you ask at reception you will be allowed to visit this great little museum for free (and almost always in a peaceful solitude that contrasts poignantly with this busy part of Canggu).

The word *puputan* is often translated as "a battle to the last man". In fact, the battles of Badung and Klungkung resulted in the death (mostly at their own hands) of as many as 4,000 Balinese men, women and children. The royal families, along with their loyal supporters, chose ritual suicide rather than surrender to the Dutch forces.

The collection in this museum includes portraits of the Balinese heroes, pieces of Ming dynasty porcelain from the wreckage of the *Sri Kumala* ship (the plundering of which triggered the Dutch invasion), and parts of a Garuda statue that were subsequently found among the ruins of the Badung Palace. There's a sculpture of the king's favourite dancer (who also killed herself during the *puputan*), and even the desk where Dutch Resident J. Eschbach wrote his letter of ultimatum to the King of Badung – which, according to local codes of honour, left so many Balinese with no effective choice other than ritual suicide. The information boards that accompany the artefacts in this museum are well presented in both English and Indonesian.

Some of the older artefacts were inherited from the owner's great grandmother (a friend of the last princess of Badung) and others were part of the cargo of the shipwrecked *Sri Kumala*. Still others were purchased on trips to Europe by Tugu's owner – lawyer, hotelier and art collector extraordinaire Anhar Setjadibrata – who had a specific desire to return precious Indonesian artwork to his native homeland.

Opposite the museum you can also visit the ornate Palace of Harmony, a Chinese temple that was originally built in 1706 and which Tugu hotel owner Anhar Setjadibrata transported here to stand as "a symbol of the harmony between the ancient Peranakan (Indonesian Chinese) and ancient Balinese cultures."

BECAK MUSEUM INDONESIA

⑨

A collection of pedicabs from across Indonesia

Losari Sunset Hotel, Jalan Merta Nadi, off Jalan Sunset Road, Kuta, Badung
0851 0660 8585
museumbecakindonesia.blogspot.com
Open 24/7

It's unlikely you'll ever see a *becak* (pronounced "be-chak") being ridden on the streets of Bali. For some reason, these often colourful cycle-trishaws never gained popularity on the island, although in recent years they have gained favour with interior designers who select these characterful cycles to grace the lobbies of hotels and restaurants. The Losari Sunset Hotel has gone a step further; instead of having just one *becak*, they have a collection from cities around Indonesia.

At first glance the Becak Museum Indonesia doesn't seem to contain much, but it really is worth hopping off busy Jalan Sunset in Kuta to learn a bit more about this form of transport that has been so popular in – and integral to the development of – cities around Indonesia.

The very first *becak* in Indonesia has been traced to the port city of Makassar on Sulawesi. In 1930 a Japanese man named Seiko San owned a bicycle shop. Business went well for a while, but when it slowed down he was left with an excess of spare parts. Seiko San tried to find an innovative way to use them, and eventually came up with a three-wheeled cycle that had seats for two passengers – and the *becak* was born. It didn't take long for the *becak* to spread into cities around Indonesia, where it became a common mode of transport for people and goods. By 1966 there were 160,000 *becak* in Jakarta alone, but in recent decades the numbers have dwindled significantly.

Jakarta, Bandung, Semarang, Yogyakarta, Surabaya, Medan, Ambon and Makassar are some of the cities that profited from this inexpensive form of transport. But what's interesting is that in most cities the design of the pedicabs evolved into something unique. In the cities on Java, for example, two passengers can sit side by side in front of the driver, and there are two wheels in front, one at the back, while in Medan the *becak* comprises two components: a bicycle and a one-wheeled carriage attached to the side of the bike. In Jakarta, the passenger seat of the *becak* was big enough to allow for two medium-sized people to sit comfortably, with space for some luggage, while in other places the *becak* are smaller, seating just one passenger. Though painting *becak* in bright colours has been common throughout Indonesia, in Yogyakarta the drivers tended to take more pride in decorating their vehicles.

As cities grow and access to motorbikes and transportation apps increases, the popularity and number of *becak* around the archipelago is on the decline. This little museum in Kuta is a wonderful tribute to a form of transport on the verge of extinction.

The origin of the word becak

At first the vehicle was called a *tiga roda* – "three wheels" – but as the pedicab became increasingly popular for the transportation of wares by Chinese merchants, people began to refer to it by the Hokkien word for "wagon", *be-chia*, and this evolved into *becak*.

Satria Bird Market: beware the real cost of exotic pets for sale

Ah, the sweet sound of birdsong, the beautiful colours of all the feathers, the cute little monkeys – and the photo opportunities. The idea of an exotic pet market might sound appealing to some travellers, but consider this: lives trapped inside cages, unhygienic conditions, and animals wrenched from the wild so regularly that their species are becoming endangered.

A visit to the Satria Bird Market (open early morning until dusk), which runs down two parallel side lanes off Jalan Veteran in central Denpasar, is unlikely to be a highlight of most Western tourists' trips to Bali, particularly those with a soft spot for wildlife. But it is important to talk about it, and to know that the market exists.

Many Indonesians keep songbirds as a hobby and endangered birds as a status symbol, but this is having a devastating effect on species in the wild. Scientists have counted 1,615 bird species – 419 of them endemic – in Indonesia, but "have found that 13 avian species and 14 additional subspecies are at risk of extinction in Sundaic Indonesia primarily as a result of trade," according to one study published in the peer-reviewed journal *Forktail*. "This is a conservative list."

The problem reaches further than "simply" a diminishing bird population: many tree species rely on birds for seed dispersal in Indonesia's rainforests, which are already under threat from deforestation.

The wildlife trade is rife in Indonesia and at the Satria market it is not just birds that are sold: there are also reptiles, fruit bats, civets, guinea fowl and monkeys. "We sell a lot of Sumatran monkeys because even when fully grown they are quite small and cute," one stallholder said. "Also, they don't bite as much as other monkeys." However, it is not unknown for traders to remove monkeys' teeth so that they cannot bite humans.

In recent years there has been pressure on authorities from organisations such as Wildlife Conservation Society Indonesia and Bali Animal Welfare Association to clamp down on the illegal wildlife trade, but when the "clean-up" of animal markets happens it seems to be on the surface only. "No, we don't sell pythons here, that is illegal," one trader at Satria Bird Market commented when we asked. After a pause the trader added, "Well, if I know in advance I might be able to source one for you."

While it might be tempting to take a selfie with a bright bird or an exotic reptile for your Instagram page, just remember that the actual cost is far, far greater than the cash you'll pay for the that photo opportunity. And remember too that purchasing the animals – no matter how noble your intentions – only creates a demand for them.

MANGROVE INFORMATION CENTRE ⑩

Preserved wetland wilderness on the outskirts of Denpasar city

Jalan Bypass Ngurah Rai, Suwung Kauh, Pemogan, Denpasar
0361 726 969
Daily 8am–5pm
Entry fee: Adults Rp200,000; children under 15, free

Of the remaining 18 million hectares of mangrove forest on our planet, an estimated 25 per cent is in Indonesia. Bali's Mangrove Information Centre near Sanur opened in 2001 with funding from Japan International Cooperation Agency; it protects about 100 hectares of this fascinating habitat.

To the uninitiated, this waterlogged forest might look monotonously repetitive, but sit still and watch for a while and you'll see that it's constantly enlivened by the jewel-like shimmer of kingfishers, the strutting form of grey herons, or the lithesome meanderings of monitor lizards. Look closer still and you'll start to appreciate the orchestral synchronicity of entire sandbanks covered with fiddler crabs and the bug-eyed timidity of mudskippers (fish that bear a great resemblance, so naturalists tell us, to our earliest ancestors). There is far more to the mangrove forests than meet the eye, and this area boasts 18 of Indonesia's 30 mangrove species.

All over Indonesia – wherever the waves permit – mangroves have formed a natural transition between the ocean and the land. A reliable source of sturdy building material and firewood, they have been denuded in many places and frequently their worth as nature's barrier to tsunamis has only been realised too late. They are a hunting place for predatory fish and a spawning ground for countless marine creatures. Their root systems trap sediment, filter nourishment and enrich the marine environment with vegetable matter. Unfortunately, in the case of this particular mangrove forest (less than 5 km from Denpasar city centre), the outgoing tide also carries with it tonnes of plastic refuse.

While the Mangrove Information Centre's 1.9 km of wooden boardwalks, watchtowers and bird hides still look good on the map, rather a lot of the infrastructure has fallen into ruin, despite the hefty entrance fee. Perhaps this fact alone illustrates what a spectacularly untameable habitat a wild mangrove forest can be. The 10.45-metres-high "Little Egret Tower" is still standing and (for the time being) the Tern Hut still offers a shady vantage point over the Gulf of Benoa, which is straddled by the 12.7 km sweep of the Mandara Toll Road.

The 8-metres-high Sun Bird Tower is dangerously dilapidated and the Spotted Dove Hut has long since given in to the advancing forest. The Pistol Shrimp Trail is now closed and the Apiculata Trail is being converted into a mini obstacle course by crumbling boardwalks and the encroaching trunks of the mangroves that apparently lent the trail its name.

"Next time you enjoy a seafood dinner, remember the mangrove"

So reads an information board near the ticket office. "We would be much poorer without them."

MADS LANGE MEMORIAL

⑪

A memorial to a Danish adventurer who loved Dalmatians

Jalan Tuan Lange, Kuta, Badung

In a Chinese cemetery down a little lane called Jalan Tuan Lange you find a unique monument – painted with black polka dots – and a statue of a spotted, blue-eyed dog that bears a startling resemblance to Perdita from Disney's *101 Dalmatians*. It was here, beside a sheltered canal just over a kilometre from Kuta beach, that a Danish adventurer by the name of Mads Lange built a trading post ... and subsequently became known to

Europeans as the "King of Bali".

Lange arrived in Bali in 1939, virtually bankrupt after losing his fortune when he backed the wrong side in a war in Lombok. He had a shrewd eye for a deal and raised money to import a shipload of *kepeng*, Chinese coins known in Bali as *pis bolong* – literally "hole coins" – that were (and still are) prized for offerings (see page 20). At that time there was no official currency and the country functioned almost exclusively on a barter system. So Lange bartered his Chinese coins for rice and promptly became Bali's first playboy entrepreneur. It is said that he was popular with the local princes as much because of his respect for traditions as for his lavish lifestyle (which featured a well-stocked wine cellar, a chamber orchestra, and a billiard table).

Lange successfully walked the line between the Dutch and Balinese, negotiating a temporary peace that won him laurels and rewards from *both* sides. He amassed a fortune trading in silk, spices, copra, tobacco, opium, weapons and slaves. He maintained a harem of concubines and two wives: one Balinese, the other a Chinese woman called Ong Sang Nio. The Chinese cemetery in "Lord Lange Lane" is the resting place of several members of the Ong family.

Lange's demise came in slow stages at first, with a rather more dramatic conclusion. A Dutch blockade of the harbour was the first disaster to hit Kuta's original thriving business, and hard on its heels came plagues of rats and smallpox, followed by a long drought. When Lange's protector, the Raja of Kesiman, went into retirement, the Danish trader realised it was time to return home after 18 years on Bali. But the raja's successor invited the 48-year-old Dane to a farewell banquet in Denpasar. It turned out to be Lange's last meal – and his 8-year-old half-Chinese daughter Cecilia (who eventually married into Malaysian royalty and whose son became the Sultan of Johor) was among those who claimed that her father was poisoned.

When Lange's tomb (which is at the site of his trading centre) was restored in 2007 for the bi-centenary of his birth, somebody had the quirky idea to not only include a *kepeng* coin motif, but to paint the stonework with the black polka dots of the Dalmatians that Lange supposedly loved so much. Locals will tell you that the many black-and-white dogs in the area are descendants of Lange's treasured pets.

TEGAL WANGI BEACH

⑫

A hidden beauty spot with a deadly side

Jalan Tegal Wangi, Jimbaran, South Kuta, Badung

Tegal Wangi – which translates as "scented backyard" or "perfumed orchard" – is one of the most dramatic parts of the abrupt Bukit Peninsula coastline. This hidden beauty spot really does feel in some ways like the backyard of the Bukit as you drive down the winding dead-end road to the rarely visited north-western corner of the peninsula. At the point where Jalan Tegal Wangi finally fades away entirely, you pull into a small gravel parking lot next to a little Pura Segara (Sea Temple).

Walk left down a narrow overgrown pathway and as soon as you step around the edge of the temple you'll be struck by views that are vertigo-inducing yet hypnotic. From the 100-metre-high cliffs you can gaze past the airport and Kuta to the great curve of Bali's westward-sweeping beaches. To the southwest you can see beyond even mightier cliffs almost to the aptly named Dreamland Beach.

Beware, however, as this deceptively idyllic seascape has a treacherous side. The cliffside track between the temple and the scrambling descent to the beach has become seriously undercut and it is unwise to walk too close to the edge. Not only that, but the sea here can be brutally fierce.

Tegal Wangi is known to a few visitors who come to enjoy the rock-pools that are converted into blissful natural Jacuzzis at low tide on calm days. On rough days the area can be a photographer's dream, and for a short while the spot garnered a fine reputation among pre-wedding photographers who knew that there was immeasurable artistic potential in the image of lovers against a backdrop of Bali's looming breakers.

In August 2015 a disaster occurred when a freak 1.5-metre wave crashed over the rock slab, dragging a Chinese bride and groom and their photographer into the water. The men were able to scramble onto the rocks but, encumbered by her wedding gown, the bride didn't make it. Her body was recovered farther along the coast an hour later.

Why green boardshorts are unlucky

According to Indonesian mythology, a goddess called Nyi Roro Kidul (Queen of the Southern Sea) is active at spots like this. Despite dating back to pre-Hindu animism, belief in her powers has remained so intact that President Sukarno even dedicated a Bali hotel room to her (see page 43). She is said to control storms and tsunamis and to protect her devotees at sea, but she also has a dark side: her favourite colour is green, and she's said to snatch young men wearing that colour and carry them to the depths of the ocean to be her lovers. Even today you'll still find young Indonesian surfers who claim that green boardshorts are unlucky.

GOA PETENG

(13)

One of Bali's most mysterious and unknown spiritual hotspots

Pura Tunjung Mekar, Jimbaran, South Kuta, Badung
0822 376 0779
Open daily – ask at the nearby house for the priest to unlock the gate
Free, but donations gratefully accepted

Until the 1970s and 1980s the Bukit Peninsula was a wild and sparsely populated place. Even today few locals can trace their lineage far back into the history of the area; Pak Wayan Katjung's family is one exception. "For longer than anyone can remember we've owned the land around Goa Peteng here on the Bukit," he says.

Wayan is the faithful retainer of what must be Bali's most spectacular and little-known cave. Despite its close proximity to several big resorts, it seems that few people, even in the neighbouring streets, know how to find the cave. Turn westwards down the unsigned coral-topped track off Jalan Goa Peteng, negotiate the rutted track for about a kilometre and – just at the stage where you wonder if your vehicle can take any more battering – you'll arrive at the gate to the little cave mouth temple. There's a small house where the priest (who keeps the keys) lives, and the back wall of a large resort looms over the little grassed parking area. The resort is also on Wayan's family land and most of the money from that lease was sunk (pardon the pun) into revamping the sacred sinkhole.

"I'll never sell this land. When I had some money I used most of it to install a cement walkway and electrical lighting into the cave," Wayan explains. The lighting (along with Wayan's old 4x4 and the rundown building that he calls his "office") has long since seen better days and you now need a torch if you intend to descend to what Wayan describes as an underground "lake" that lies an estimated 150 metres away under the dusty thorn scrub of the Bukit. Local legends claim that when the tide is at its lowest it's possible to pass from this chamber into another tunnel that eventually emerges at the beach. Wayan refutes this, however. "That would be the best part of a kilometre," he says, "and anyway the water in the sinkhole is fresh, not salty. It doesn't seem to be affected by the tide at all and you can always swim there."

Wayan has rarely seen snakes in the cave, but the floor is thick with centuries' worth of guano from countless bats. We visited during a spell of unusually powerful seismic activity, so it seemed inadvisable to descend far into the bowels of the earth. But Wayan claims that his team was once working deep in the tunnel during an earthquake. "It was scary," he recalls, "but we were working for the spirits of the cave so nothing bad happened."

The porous subterranean reefs of the Bukit Peninsula are probably riddled with undiscovered caves, but for the moment it seems only Goa Peteng has been explored. While swarms of tourists seem to outnumber even the famous bats at the cave temple of Goa Lawah (near Padangbai), the Bukit's enigmatic Goa Peteng remains one of Bali's most mysterious and unknown spiritual hotspots.

NUSA DUA'S NATURAL BLOWHOLE

14

An untamed reminder of the power of the south seas

Benoa, South Kuta, Badung

It can be a refreshing experience to see a little touch of tropical savagery vent its power against the man-made luxury holiday haven of Nusa Dua. Just stand back and watch from a safe distance as the might of the ocean forces itself into a narrow lava chamber to jet skywards with all the force of a breaching whale. This is the most invigorating natural show in Nusa Dua, and here, between the manicured lawns and hotel shuttle buggies, it comes as a breath of fresh (and often very salty) air.

Known in geological terms as a "marine geyser", this blowhole is caused when hydraulic pressure from waves and tide blasts water through a narrow opening in the lava field that spills onto the coastline. In some cases the air coming out of blowholes has been measured in excess of 70km/hr, and the Nusa Dua blowhole (which frequently jets water 4 metres or more into the air) is clearly no weakling.

The blowhole is on the tip of a small peninsula at the far eastern point of the Bukit Peninsula (between the Grand Hyatt and the Melia Bali resorts). The inlet is so positioned to take the full force of the southerly swell, which is barricaded from the resort beaches by the natural barrier reef that is no doubt a factor in the founding of the resorts in the first place.

Nusa Dua was established in the 1970s as an all-inclusive holiday package destination and is now home to more than 20 large-scale resorts. Nevertheless, it is still very much a work in progress; the area around the blowhole is currently being developed by the Indonesia Tourism Development Corporation and access to the platform overlooking the blowhole is now across a building site. If the waves are powerful it is sensible to stay alert as you walk along the concrete pathway because the blowhole is curiously erratic and might often be misleadingly tame for as long as 20 minutes before catching you unawares with a particularly violent (and drenching) blast.

The room that miraculously escaped a great fire

In any other city, the Grand Inna Bali Beach hotel would look like just another holiday resort. But in Bali, this nine-storey building stands out as the tallest building on the island by far (the Bali Beach Hotel – as it was known then – was completed in 1967, but in 1970 Bali Province passed a law that no building, except towers of religious buildings, electrical towers, lighthouses and aviation buildings, may exceed a height of 15 metres or be taller than the palm trees; that law still stands today). And while it looks like a cut-and-paste hotel property, it is (unintentionally) filled with intrigue.

The hotel was built by Sukarno (see page 18), the first president of Indonesia, with reparation funds from the Japanese after World War II. Bung Karno, as the ex-president was affectionately known, was a firm believer in the spiritual realm and it is said that he promised to dedicate a part of the property to Nyi Roro Kidul, the mythical queen of the Southern Sea (the Indian Ocean). In 1966, before the hotel was complete, Bung Karno was stripped of his presidency and he never fulfilled his promise to the queen.

Fast forward to 20 January 1993 when a fire broke out in the hotel. It was so severe that it was three days before firefighters were able to enter the building to assess the damage. Damage to the property was extensive and every room in the hotel's main building was destroyed – except for room number 327, which remained completely untouched by the fire. The heat was so intense that the metal railings on the rooms surrounding room 327 melted, but in that particular room, even the curtains and plastic telephone remained in pristine condition.

It soon became widely accepted that the queen of the Southern Sea had watched over room 327; some say she had come to claim the room that she was promised by Bung Karno. The room became a shrine to Nyi Roro Kidul and has not been rented out since the fire. It remains locked and, to this day, offerings are made daily to the queen.

We found it impossible to get access to the room and near impossible to get staff to tell us about it. "Room 327 did survive the fire, yes," a manager who has worked at the hotel for more than 20 years eventually admitted. "I am not permitted to show you, but I will say that every day someone from senior staff will take fresh flowers and make offerings in the room."

Photos of room 327 do exist online. The room is predominantly green, the favourite colour of the sea goddess: ornate green wallpaper, green linen and carpets, green and gold curtains, and the centre piece of the shrine, a large painting of Nyi Roro Kidul, very similar to one hanging in the Museum Bung Karno. Those who have been into the room say that it has a very definite mysterious, spiritual atmosphere.

MELASTI BEACH

⑮

The most southerly point in western Indonesia

Ungasan, South Kuta, Badung

The road to Bali's most southerly tip might be the most spectacular civil engineering project on the island – yet it leads to virtually nothing. For some reason (and at unimaginable expense), a colossal switchback highway has been carved through a series of cliffs that rear up to 80 metres alongside the road. At the bottom, a man-made causeway inexplicably extends the island beyond a couple of lackadaisical beach bars a further 200 metres into the South Bali Sea. Few people ever bother to walk to the southern extreme of the island, so if you stroll out here to the end of the point you'll be the most southerly person in the whole of western Indonesia.

Perhaps the road was designed specifically to establish Melasti's position as a sort of pre-wedding fashion-show catwalk; on any day you might see shimmering white bridal gowns fluttering in the trade winds like maritime symbols of surrender. Be-suited and be-sodden, grooms mop their foreheads as the sun sears down the fabricated canyons and white satin pumps struggle to maintain traction among slippery rock pools. There's even a small industry for people who rent out classic cars as backdrops to the pre-wedding shoots.

It's no wonder that these chiffon flamingos flock here in such numbers. Melasti Beach has the sort of postcard beauty that makes it imminently Instagrammable – at least if you follow the rules of the pros and keep the camera focussed away from the stalled bulldozers and mechanical hardware of what seems to be another Bukit building project on the backburner.

If you take a different view – look through a sort of soft-focus filter – you can imagine how this beautiful spot might have appeared to the first visitors who set eyes on it. The southern waves still rumble along the edge of a coral lagoon and the white sand beach is brightened by a few vibrantly painted *jukung* fishing boats (almost certainly rigged for netting wedding couples rather than fish).

Walk or drive westwards along the gravel beach road for just 400 metres and you'll find a second little cove with a couple of *warungs* and a score of rented parasols. Some travellers rave that this is the best beach on the Bukit Peninsula. The sand is gleaming white and the offshore barrier reef protects a turquoise lagoon that makes for perfect swimming. Strangely, few of the pre-wedding photographers seem to aim their cameras around this prettier side of the headland.

EAST JAVA
Menjangan Island
West Bali National Park
Pemuteran
Labuhan Lalang
Gilimanuk
Sumberklampok
Cekik
Banyuwangi
Belimbingsari
Pala Sari Reservoir
WES
Bali Strait
Negara
Pengambengan
Perancak
N
0
10 km

West Bali

Singaraja
BALI SEA
NORTH BALI
Tegallenga
Seririt
S. Saba
Lake Buyan
Lake Tamblingan
Lake Bratan
Pupuan
Batukaru 2276m
Pekutatan
Gumbrih
CENTRAL BALI
Balian
Antap

SOKA RICE TERRACES

1

The most beautiful secret paddies on the island

Jalan Raya Denpasar-Gilimanuk, between Soka and Antap villages, Tabanan

A great sweeping vista of rice paddies ripples across the natural contours of the hillside like the fingerprints of the gods. This is quite possibly Bali's most spectacular expanse of terraces, yet few tourists ever even come this far west, where a vast, almost unbroken staircase of paddies descends nearly 5 km from the foothills of Batukaru mountain to the beach at Soka. Another stretch of paddies sprawls a solid kilometre from the eastern bank of the river that runs through the village of Antap.

The most photographed rice paddies in Bali are probably those at Tegalalang, near Ubud. While they are spectacular, their coverage (barely 500 metres wide) is miniscule compared with the great swirling patchwork blanket of paddies at Soka. Even the famous terraces at Jatiluwih (a Unesco candidate) fall short of Soka's sprawling immensity.

It's often said that the Inuit people have 50 words for snow, and when it comes to rice, Indonesians aren't too far behind: cooked rice is *nasi*; before cooking it's called *beras*; when still on the plant it's *padi*. The word "paddy" has been anglicised to refer to the actual terraces, but the Balinese refer to the fields as *sawah*.

The *sawah* is constantly in flux, changing dramatically from week to week, but it is sometimes possible to witness almost the entire cycle as you drive past the stretch of terraces near Soka. In some places the fields will have been harvested and will be gleaming like mirrors, their watery surface broken only by a few uncut stems. Close by, another section will almost have reached the 90 days that rice takes to mature.

Swirling flocks of birds will be gathering to raid the crops, and the farmers will be busy erecting wind-operated mechanical scarecrows and weaving webs of flapping plastic to scare the winged marauders, so that something might be left on the plants when the harvesting teams arrive from Java. These immigrant workers cross by ferry from their East Java homes to spend a month moving from harvest to harvest while they live in shanty towns rigged from plastic sheets. Working for the local landowners, these men and women might only make about US $6 a day. It's a rate that most comparatively wealthy Balinese would refuse, but the island's rice harvests (falling three times per year) offer enough work to entice hundreds of migrant labourers from neighbouring islands.

GOA MARIA SHRINE AT SELABIH ②

A shrine with heavenly views

Unnamed Road, Selabih, Selemadeg Barat, Tabanan
Daily, church open only on Sundays
Free, donations gratefully accepted

A signpost marked "Goa Maria Selabih" lures you off the main road along the southern coast of west Bali. It's less than 2 km uphill to the little chapel, but the road climbs so steeply that you feel the drop in

temperature as you wind through clove and cacao forests. The strange fruits that hang like new potatoes from the trees are locally known as *sawo* ("sapodilla plum" in English). Known these days as an agricultural speciality of Selabih, *sawo* originates from Central America and was imported to Asia by the Spanish.

This is not the only Latin import that seems to have borne fruit: Selabih is one of Bali's few Catholic enclaves. The little parish church (which will be locked unless it's Sunday) at the top of the hill is an intriguing combination of Western Christian architecture and traditional Balinese trimmings. Behind the church a surprise awaits.

Goa Maria (often spelled Gua Maria) literally means "Maria's Cave" and refers to an outdoor shrine to the Virgin Mary. Surrounded by tropical vegetation and a tinkling water feature, the Goa Maria at Selabih is perhaps the most beautifully situated on the island, offering views over palm plantations towards Bali's wild west coast.

In Indonesia "Goa Maria" usually designates a series of monuments relating to the Stations of the Cross, which the Christian congregation follows during the Easter procession in commemoration of the path that Jesus took during the day of crucifixion. One of these locations can be visited at Goa Maria Ratu Gumbrih (just 7 km west of Selabih in Gumbrih village), but the island's most spectacular example is just uphill from the Sacred Heart of Jesus Catholic Church at Palasari (see page 88).

Christianity's first disastrous forays into the Island of the Gods

Efforts to convert the Balinese to Catholicism began with a letter from the Raja of Klungkung (written on lontar palm in 1635, which is now in the Vatican library) inviting the church to send priests from the Portuguese colony in Melaka. There were many false starts, and the Balinese clung so firmly to their traditional religion that it wasn't until 238 years later that a missionary called Jacob de Vroom baptised the first Balinese person. His name was Gusti Wayan Karangasen and he was baptised simply as Nicedemus. In 1867 De Vroom wrote to his organisation that "evangelism in Bali was exceedingly difficult" – and before the end of that year his first convert had murdered him. The newly reborn Nicedemus was finally hanged for the murder.

The subsequent ban on Christian missionary work in Bali lasted for 70 years, but it seems that by then, the time was ripe: sources from this period claimed that within two years 115 Balinese people had been baptised.

YEH LEH BEACH

③

More than 10 km of empty black sand beach

Very few "surfaris" ever reach beyond the west Bali surf hamlet of Balian. Another 5 km west from here – along the highway to Gilimanuk – you find a surf break that is known to just a few local surfers as Truckstop. Immediately after the rocky headland at Truckstop there's a section of the coast that not many people (foreigners or local) ever lay their eyes upon. From here, a wild, palm-shaded beach stretches unbroken for more than 10 km to the town of Pekutatan. There are a few villages along the highway, but due to traditional Balinese taboos against living on the beaches, this great arcing strip of sand, buffeted by un-surfed South Bali Sea breakers, remains virtually deserted.

With a suitable vehicle you can drive or ride along this beach, but take care not to get caught by the incoming tide. And bear in mind that this coast remains a popular nesting ground for turtles – spinning tyres can wreak havoc in the nesting zone above the high tide line.

At low tide, if you drop down onto the sand near the little temple (100 metres west of the buffalo racing monument at Truckstop), you'll be able to ride a motorbike right along the sand. If the river before Medewi is dry enough, you can even reach the "haunted beach" (see page 68).

Along this beach at sunset – with the volcanoes of Java silhouetted on the horizon – you're likely to see more kingfishers than people. If this were a white sand beach, then this area would undoubtedly already have gone the way of Nusa Dua-style development. Thankfully, the hot black volcanic sand means that this shimmering beach has avoided the fate that has befallen so much of the island's coastline.

Apart from a handful of fishermen, there is one small industry here. Towards the western end of this arc of sand there is a small inlet where a small team of up to a dozen men (and sometimes women) work to shovel the black sand into panniers on the backs of motorbikes. This sand, considered particularly sacred from this river mouth spot, is used in the construction of temples and shrines in the area.

BALI REPTILE RESCUE CENTRE

4

Rescue, research and release centre for wildlife

Jalan Taman, Gumbrih, Pekutatan, Jembrana
0821 4638 0270
Open 24 hours for emergencies or removal of reptiles from property; 8am–6pm for visits
Free, donations gratefully received

My brother Putu had captured a king cobra from a home up in the hills and was bringing it back to the rescue centre," Kadek Ray recalls. "They say he slipped and fell. He must have relaxed his grip on the snake's head for a moment because afterwards there was just a small fang mark in the end of one finger." I Putu Agus Edi Darmawan was dead within half an hour.

Some people might imagine that such a tragedy so close to home would lessen a person's enthusiasm for the reptile world, but Kadek Ray runs his Bali Reptile Rescue team with a devotion that is obvious from the moment you meet him. Bali has 43 snake species and there are usually around 15 to 20 snakes in the cages here, ranging from the delicate blue viper (like a sliver of cloudless Balinese sky) to a 5-metre-long king cobra.

Ray is happy to let visitors handle relatively harmless inmates like the appropriately named *ular pelangi* (rainbow snake), the lovely carpet snake and even a 3-metre-long python weighing in at 45 kg. Don't let the humble little family compound fool you into thinking this is just some sort of petting zoo, however; Ray's expert knowledge has wowed viewers on Discovery Channel and his rescue centre has won the backing of the Bali Zoo and Bali Bird Park.

The centre frequently removes snakes from hotels, resorts and homes, and is known locally as the emergency go-to point in the case of venomous bites (usually from pit vipers in this area).

"People often still have a habit of resorting to traditional medicine to deal with snakes," Ray explains. "For example, there's a belief that if you can get hold of a bronzeback snake – which are fairly common here and grow up to about 1.2 metres – you should actually *let it bite you*. People believe that this will give you immunity." Even the most misguided traditions often derive some semblance of logic, and Ray explains that the bronzeback, while not venomous, is actually toxic to other snakes: "If a king cobra eats a bronzeback, the cobra will die," he says.

The centre does not restrict its activities solely to the reptile kingdom. While Ray delicately peels a tick from the chin of an albino python his wife is busy feeding mashed banana to an orphaned baby civet. You're likely to see macaques (confiscated from dealers), palm civets (rescued prisoners of the *kopi luwak* – civet coffee – industry), Balinese civets (too small for effective *kopi luwak* exploitation), flying foxes with broken wings, small crocodiles, and a porcupine or two.

The undisputed local stars, however, are the deadly king cobras – one of which measures almost 5 metres. Ray has been known to hold the cage door wide open to allow dedicated photographers to get that unforgettable eye-contact portrait of a rearing cobra.

JUWUK MANIS WATERFALL
⑤

A mini expedition to west Bali's twin cascade

Manggissari, Pekutatan, Jembrana
Free, donations welcome

Getting to Manggissari village is half the fun of an excursion to west Bali's prettiest waterfall. From Pangyangan village (on the busy Denpasar-Gilimanuk road) the "road less travelled" takes you on a steep climb towards the barely explored highlands of the "wild west". You drive alongside a government research centre for the breeding of Balinese cattle before one of the loveliest roads in Bali weaves an enchanting course between semi-wild rubber plantations to the left and scented clove forests to the right. From here you climb to a dramatic ridge – with 100-metre-high drops on either side – that is still clad in dense jungle. Beyond the hilltop temple of Pura Kawitan Taman Giri the road continues to weave steeply upwards through coffee plantations in a series of switchbacks until you reach Manggissari (about 9 km from the coast).

Compared with the crowded waterfall treks of central and north Bali, this area rarely sees visitors and you can simply park alongside the road in the village before heading down a narrow alleyway towards the trailhead. Now comes the second half of the fun: a steep descent of 868 steps to the waterfall itself.

The trail, which used to become so slippery after rains as to be almost impassable, has been improved in recent years, and the concrete walkway (with steel railings for much of the way) makes it much safer and allows for opportunities to observe wild orchids and the myriad butterflies that flit through the undergrowth. The bottom section can still be slippery, however, since the damp forest here – shimmering with water and dripping with cloud forest mosses – is irrigated permanently by the falls.

The 8-metres-high waterfall is far from the most dramatic in Bali. But the spot is a pretty one, and since there's very little habitation upriver from here, the water is clean; silt from natural jungle run-off can sometimes make it murky after rain, but this is a wonderful place to swim and picnic. There are no facilities here so bring snacks and drinking water.

Unfortunately, since the improvement of the trail has made the falls more accessible, some visitors have seen no need to make the uphill climb with their garbage, and plastic refuse has increased along the banks below the falls. There's a box for donations at the top of the trail and it is to be hoped that some of that money goes towards keeping the falls clean.

The kilometre-long hike back up the trail can be heavy going on a hot afternoon, but for anyone with average fitness it is easily doable. For added motivation, focus on the fact that just across the street at the top there is a small *warung* selling cold drinks and ice creams. Rather than return by the same route, you can take a scenic drive back via Bunut Bulong (see page 58) and an equally beautiful descent to the coast road at Pekutatan.

THE TABOOS OF BUNUT BOLONG ⑥

Would you dare to drive through the tunnel in a sacred fig tree?

Jalan Pekutatan, Manggisari, Pekutatan, Jembrana

A highlight on the beautiful road that runs north to south across West Bali is Bunut Bolong, a fig tree that has formed a tunnel over the road. Grab a coffee at the tree-side *warung* and watch as a stream of motorbikes, cars and lorries pass through the tree. You may notice that some vehicles take the bypass road around the trunk – this is because there are certain taboos regarding passage through Bunut Bulong.

It is said that anyone "unclean" may not pass through the sacred tree. In Balinese Hinduism, for example, mothers and their babies are considered unclean for 42 days after birth, and even people en route to a ceremony (and therefore yet to be blessed) might be considered unclean. More strictly, bodies of deceased people being taken for cremation should not pass through the tree.

Locals explain that Bunut Bulong should be viewed as a great *candi bentar* (split gate entrance to a temple). A Balinese Hindu would consider it wicked to pass through a *candi bentar* without first elevating their mind to a more spiritual plane. In the same way, many feel uneasy about passing through the tunnel without paying respect to the sacred tree first.

The shrine at Bunut Bulong is permanently laden with offerings, and the fact that the bypass lane has recently been repaved is further evidence that the taboos are still in effect. There is another unusual myth concerning this old fig tree: it is said that courting couples should not pass through the tree before they have been married. To do so would bring a curse upon their relationship.

Beginning at Pekutatan on the southern coastline, the road that passes through Bunut Bulong winds up through plantations of palm, rubber, coffee, cacao and clove trees; just after picking season the air is perfumed with the scent of drying cloves. It leads over a spine of mountains then drops through tunnels of trees to the flatlands of Seririt on the north coast. The most picturesque time to drive this road is just after sunrise when mist rises from the creases of densely forested valleys; incense wafts from shrines, and the sun's low rays add a luminescence to roadside flowers. Near Pupuan there are excellent views of Batukaru, Bali's second highest mountain. Later in the day this view fades into haze, but in the early morning, the outlook across paddies and plantations towards the volcanic peak is remarkable.

PULUKAN STATE PLANTATION ⑦

See traditional rubber-making methods at Bali's only colonial-era rubber plantation

Jalan Pekutatan, Asahduren, Pekutatan, Jembrana
While it's possible to drop in (if you make a donation) you're only likely to get a meaningful understanding of the rubber industry through a guided tour such as the one run by local Puri Dajuma resort: www.dajuma.com
Daily 8am–5pm

Pulukan State Plantation (just north of Pekutatan village) boasts 800 hectares of rubber forests, where there are an estimated 65,000 rubber trees surrounding what is said to be the only remaining colonial-era rubber plant in Bali. The plantation was established under Dutch administration in the 1930s and fell into Japanese hands during World War II. Apart from some minor mechanisation, little has changed during the decades and the natural latex is still harvested and prepared in much the same way as it always was. This evocatively historical production plant, where each day two tons of white natural latex is prepared for later conversion into vehicle tyres and other products, is the perfect place to see the process in action.

One hundred and thirteen people work in the plantation, warehouses and smoking rooms here. Each plantation worker collects the solidified white sap from about 400 trees every day, rotating through his crop so that each tree receives a fresh diagonal slice into the bark every three days. The rubber is then mixed with water and acid, causing it to liquefy, before being poured into a huge trough, segregated with metal plates, so that after 24 hours of setting time, thick pillow-like sheets of rubber can be taken out and forced through a mechanical press to flatten them.

Next the sheets are hung to drip for 24 hours before going into one of several smoking rooms (like oversized ovens) where the rubber is smoked for four days at 60 degrees Celsius. The slow fires are fuelled with timber from rubber trees that have surpassed their 35-year productive lifespan, making this a surprisingly ecological production process for such a toxic end product.

Indonesia is the world's second biggest rubber producer (after Thailand), with about 3.5 million hectares being farmed throughout the country, mostly in Sumatra and Java. More than 3 million metric tons are produced each year, mostly by small-scale farmers in a process that is almost identical to that used at Pulukan State Plantation (except that the press is usually hand-operated – just like an old-time clothes mangle).

A gentle stroll through the rubber plantations – instantly recognisable from the diagonal slices in the trunks – can be a fascinating experience if you are in the company of a knowledgeable and enthusiastic guide. The plantations in this part of Bali (whether cacao, coffee, clove or snake fruit) are diverse semi-wild habitats where medicinal plants are gathered along with the primary crop.

FISHING BOATS ON PEKUTATAN BEACH

(8)

A colourful collection of Bali's unique outriggers

Pantai Pekutatan, Jalan Pelabuhan, Pekutatan, Jembrana

You'll see outrigger fishing boats (known locally as *jukung*) in various parts of Bali but they're rarely as dramatic as the ones in the traditional fishing fleets that tackle the big waves off Pekutatan and Medewi beaches. There are only a handful of artisans in these communities who still create the sleek timber craft, but along a 2-km-long stretch of coastline you'll find a fleet of about 150 of what must be some of the world's finest traditional timber outrigger boats. When not out at sea these spectacular boats are hauled up onto the beach, where they rest in the shade of palm trees.

These elegant, handcrafted 7-metre-long *jukungs* (best seen at Pekutatan) still preserve most of their traditional appearance, despite the fact that these days they are powered by the Thai Kipor engines that are common on the longtail boats of Bangkok. With luck, a *jukung* might survive 10 years here on the rocky, wave-smashed coast of west Bali. But these days only two families in Pekutatan have the knowledge to build from scratch. These vessels take about a month to build, using five different types of wood, and cost about Rp18 million.

In Amed (on Bali's north-east coast), *jukungs* are smaller and – without a powerful swell to battle with – they still frequently travel under sail. In Negara, motorised *jukung* are often mounted with symbolic Islamic domes, and in Sanur the bow is carved into the gaping mouth and wide eyes of what looks like a startled marlin.

Many of Pekutatan's fishing fleet are still rigged with sweeping crossbars of several brightly painted bamboos (sometimes as many as five) lofted high like an elongated boom. Apart from being a support for a shade cloth in still weather, they serve little purpose and are primarily there as a reminder of what these boats looked like back in the days when they still carried sails. The slender stern mast is still known as the *tangan layar* (literally the "hand of the sail") and is frequently mounted with a carved effigy of what at first glance appears to be a snarling dog. In fact, it is known as a *menjangan*, and despite the elongated fangs, these are representations of the Timor deer *(Cervus timorensis)*, the animal that lent its name to Menjangan Island, now a well-known dive spot 90 minutes to the north-west of Pekutatan.

Timor deer swim well and it is said that they are so well adapted to coastal life that they drink seawater. About half of Pekutatan's fishermen hail from Muslim regions. But regardless of religious affiliations, the *menjangan* effigies are a common addition to a *jukung's* spiritual rigging. It is possible that this is another Balinese tradition that might predate the arrival of both Hinduism and Islam.

"Nobody can remember why we do these things," says Pekutatan boatwright Pak Hor as he puts the finishing touches to a boat that has been named *Mutiara Laut* (*Sea Pearl*). "Just as it would be foolish to go to sea without waiting for the elders to confirm a good day, or making the necessary offerings, many people consider that a boat is not fully equipped without a *menjangan* to protect it."

NGURAH RAI MONUMENT

9

An unusual concrete boat that commemorates Indonesia's own Che Guevara

Pekutatan beach, Jalan Pelabuhan, Pekutatan, Jembrana

Officially known as Monumen Pendaratan I Gusti Ngurah Rai, this unusual concrete boat commemorates the landing of Independence hero I Gusti Ngurah Rai. The freedom fighter's name might sound familiar to anyone who has arrived at Bali's international airport ... and you may well be carrying a portrait of him around in your wallet in the form of a Rp50,000 note.

This concrete boat on the beach in Pekutatan marks the spot where Lieutenant Colonel Ngurah Rai landed on 4 April 1946 to lead Bali in the fight for national freedom. Symbolically, one of the concrete figures on the boat is in the act of picking up an ammunition case, and although Ngurah Rai must have arrived with a larger force than this little crew of three, it is said that his troops were bringing extra ammunition and arms to reinforce the various beleaguered and divided Balinese guerrilla factions.

Born in Carangsari (central Bali), Ngurah Rai was trained by the Dutch Army at the Reserve Officer Training Corps in Magalang, Java. In April 1946 he returned to his home island from Yogyakarta (the republican capital) to confront an army of 2,000 Dutch soldiers, on which he inflicted defeats in several skirmishes near Tabanan. The Dutch, backed up by air strikes and troops from Lombok, retaliated with a brutal attack that wiped out his entire force.

A few years ago the monument was falling to pieces under the buffeting of (frequently very powerful) south coast waves. The concrete figures of freedom fighters were toppling and one lay face down in a nearby rock pool. It has since been renovated, and is often decked with flags by the nearby Puri Dajuma eco-resort (an ideal place to grab a lunch or sundowner and from where to watch the waves breaking over the monument).

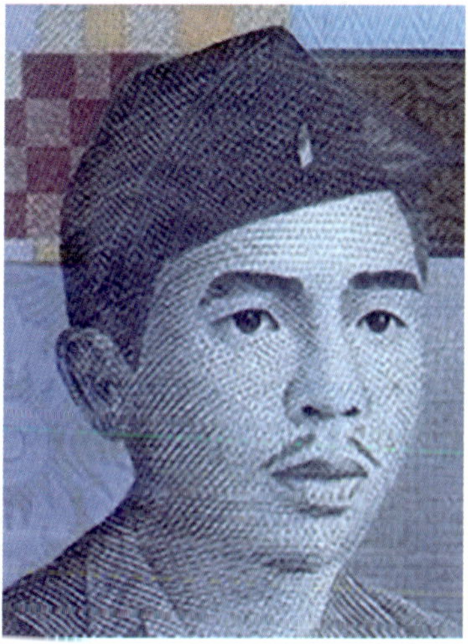

Within seven months of landing in Pekutatan, the 29-year-old freedom fighter was killed, along with 97 men, when he ordered a ritual *puputan* (a fight to the death) in the Battle of Margarana (see page 220). I Gusti Ngurah Rai was posthumously promoted to Brigadier General, but it was not until 1975 that he was declared a national hero.

MEDEWI'S HAUNTED BEACH

⑩

Local legend has it that the black sand here has healing power

Medewi Beach, Jembrana

Surfers pass by with eyes only for the peeling waves of Medewi's celebrated point break, while at their backs, soaring coconut palms loom over one of the most mystical spots on the Island of the Gods.

"Some people say that here they've seen a ghostly old woman dressed in white and with hair that reaches to the ground," says local healer Pak Nasri. "Occasionally, on a moonlit night, I've seen a ghost palace silhouetted among the rocks near the river mouth."

Tales of ghost sightings (even occasionally by travellers) abound, but this place is said to be very positively spiritual rather than evil. This little stretch of beach – wedged between a hotel and a river mouth – has always been considered a place of importance by members of both the Hindu and Muslim communities in this part of Bali. Ceremonies are sometimes held here with up to 200 Hindu worshippers driving down the dirt track that leads here through a tiny fishing village.

Occasionally you'll meet people who have travelled from the surrounding villages to cover rheumatic limbs with the black volcanic sand that they believe has healing qualities. If the towering coconut palms (among the tallest on the island) are anything to go by then there may indeed be something inherently powerful about this place.

Why you should not whistle while strolling along a beach at night

The Balinese may well be unique among the world's islanders for their inherent fear of the sea, and even of their beautiful beaches. The coastline was long believed to be the haunt of evil spirits, and even today few traditional Balinese would enjoy a walk on the sand after sunset. If you do find yourself strolling at night along a beach with nervous Balinese friends, don't try to reassure them with hearty whistling; many Balinese still believe that whistling is a way to summon evil spirits.

DUCK HERDERS AT THE PULUKAN RICE PADDIES ⑪

There is more to duck herding than meets the eye

Pulukan, Jembrana
In Pulukan, take any turning off Jalan Raya Denpasar-Gilimanuk towards the coast and you'll come to the rice paddies

The beautiful expanse of paddies between the main road and the beach at Pulukan really is a sight to behold. If you arrive later in the rice-growing season you'll see a verdant green "carpet" that stretches out towards the Indian Ocean – it's truly spectacular, particularly in the early mornings and late afternoons. Just after harvesting (there are usually three harvests in a year), the landscape at first appears less vibrant. But look a little closer and you'll see, in different paddies, hundreds of ducks quacking their way through the waterlogged fields.

The ducks aerate the soil with their webbed feet and add fertiliser; they collect the last grains of rice, along with algae and insects, and feed on the voracious yellow snails that farmers say arrived in west Bali from Java during the past decade.

As with so many things on this spiritual island, there is more to the ducks than meets the eye. *Pengangon bebek* (duck herders) are frequently seen in the paddies around Pulukan; like Balinese pied pipers they usher their flocks through the harvested paddies, bringing the sound of cheerful quacking to sunlit equatorial mornings. *Pengangon bebek* are often seen in rice-farming areas throughout the island, but to paddy workers around Pulukan village the herders are still considered to be the inheritors of ancient magical powers. The *penyisih* staffs they carry – traditionally a long, feather-tipped piece of bamboo with a white cloth flag halfway up – were handed down from generation to generation, and many people still claim they are invested with magical spirits. "An evil or jealous person could ruin the entire flock just by touching that stick," one Balinese farmer explained. "Just by touching it he could stop all the ducks from laying, and by shaking it he could create havoc among the flock."

The ducks are usually herded for the night into a temporary fenced compound with a tarpaulin shelter in a paddy, and the magical staff is stuck into the ground overnight to protect them. Foreigners are often surprised by how low the fence is, but Balinese ducks have evolved into birds that are less adept at flight even than chickens; as a tropical species they have no need to migrate.

DEWI SRI SHRINES AT MENDAJA (12)

Fertility shrines that predate the arrival of Hinduism in Bali

South of Jalan Raya Denpasar-Gilimanuk, a huge paddy tract marked on maps as Mendaja (ask direction towards Delod Brawah or Perancak)

Shrines to the goddess Dewi Sri come in various shapes and sizes, but when you come across a stone or concrete shrine in the rice paddies you can be fairly certain that it was built in homage to the goddess who probably far predates the arrival of Hinduism on this island. You'll see these stone shrines in the rice fields all over Bali, but the paddies on the coastal plains south of Negara (a beautiful emerald savannah stretching about 5 kilometres) are easily accessible, making this a wonderful place to explore more closely. Farther east, most coastal paddies have long since been taken over for tourism development and only the steeper inland paddies remain – but here on the west coast you are able to walk among the paddies with ease.

Most visitors assume that the paddy shrines are further manifestations of Bali's Hindu religion, but Dewi Sri is an ancient goddess of fertility who might date back to the beginning of rice cultivation in Indonesia (wild rice was probably already being harvested in Sulawesi around 3000 BC). These days, Dewi Sri is often associated with the Hindu goddess Lakshmi (benefactor of prosperity), but few Balinese are likely to enter into such theological discussions; they will simply tell you that only a fool would try to plant rice on Bali without paying homage to Dewi Sri.

The paddy workers you see labouring in the fields are rarely land-owners themselves but are growing the rice as tenant farmers; after the harvest has been gathered and all expenses covered, the landowner will share the profits with them. Likewise, the Balinese workers will often hand the heavy task of harvesting over to migrant teams from Java who move from harvest to harvest while they live in shanty towns rigged from plastic sheets.

Bali's ancient Subak system

The main reason for Bali's agricultural success has always been the local Subak, the ancient councils of elders that coordinate and control the activities of local groups of farmers. A democratically managed law-enforcement agency that stipulates when to plough, plant and harvest in each area, the Subak has traditionally guaranteed that everybody gets their rightful share of the sacred water that is the lifeblood of the island. A thousand years of experience qualifies the Subaks to dictate which other crops (such as beans, watermelon or corn) should be raised periodically in order to rejuvenate the sawah terraces and conserve water.

The Subak system is so successful that over in Java they also tried to replicate it. "It didn't work so well there, of course," the Balinese point out, "because nobody observed the crucial offerings and ceremonies for Dewi Sri."

The Subak system is recognised by Unesco as a Cultural Landscape of Bali.

FISHING BOATS OF PERANCAK

13

The fishing fleet that looks like a floating art gallery

Air Kuning inlet, Perancak, Negara, Jembrana
Turn south off the main Denpasar-Gilimanuk road at the village of Tegal Cangkring. Follow Jalan Sekar Jagat 2 km towards the beach, then turn right and stick to the Yeh Kuning coast road for about 8 km

Appearing at first glance like a fleet of psychedelic Viking longboats, the boats of Perancak are among the world's most spectacular traditional fishing craft. Each one is about 20 metres long and their great looming bows rise to about 8 metres above the mirror-like waters of the inlet. What makes them look even more like Viking longboats are what seem to be rows of oars held suspended at the ready above the water. But rather than oars powered by barbarian plunderers, these are long-shafted propellers, each driven by a diesel motor (often six per boat) mounted along the gunwales to provide impressive power and manoeuvrability.

There are an estimated 150 vibrantly painted, timber-hulled trawlers along this part of the coastline. If this glittering armada were in east Bali it would be a major tourist sight, but here in west Bali you're unlikely to see another foreign face.

These boats, called *perahu selerek*, carry crews of up to 20. They come from Madura (an island north of Java), but even there you rarely find traditional teak boats of this scale and splendour. There is clearly a huge amount of pride of ownership in these vessels, and maintenance is so rigorous that you rarely see one with chipping, faded paintwork or tattered banners.

The best time to come is early morning to coincide with the off-loading of the boats. Then the sleepy little beach is thronging with chattering people, and the usually deserted lane is bustling with pickup trucks and panier-bearing mopeds ready to make the rush to canning factories and fish markets across Bali.

One of the most noticeable aspects of the Perancak fleet is that the *perahu selerek* are almost always moored in matching pairs. *Selerek* refers to the purse-seine fishing technique. The "male" and "female" boats each play such a vital part in the technique that on the rare occasion a boat is forced to work alone, it is known locally as a *janda* – a widow.

Look closer still and you'll notice that while both boats have the brightly painted bamboo spars known as *belandang* (traditionally used to dry nets, but now purely decorative), the foremast of the slightly smaller "female" boat will be topped with what looks like a vibrantly decorated "throne room". What would pass as a humble crow's nest in other boats is often styled (depending on the owner's tastes or religious sensibilities) to appear either as an Islamic throne, decorated with the guardian image of a Muslim saint, or as what might appear to be a magical toy motorcar. It actually represents the royal chariot that, in Hindu mythology, carried Prince Rama into battle.

PENGAMBENGAN HARBOUR

14

An outrageously colourful fishing harbour

Jalan Raya Pengambengan, Pengambengan, Jembrana

Pengambengan Harbour, across the paddies and about 7 kilometres south of Negara city centre, is a classic working fishing harbour that looks like it could be part of a vibrant floating carnival. Apart from several hundred *jukung* outrigger fishing boats (many mounted with symbolic Islamic domes on the bow mast), you'll see a great fleet of brightly painted 20-metre-long traditional timber trawlers.

While some of this fleet of about 150 boats can be seen at the pretty Perancak inlet (see page 74), you are likely to see as many as 100 in Pengambengan harbour at one time. It is extremely rare that a tourist ventures into the harbour so you are likely to catch a lot of interest from fishermen, porters and maintenance crews.

The boats are known as *perahu selerek*, and although they are built on Madura island (north of Java), this is the largest fleet of these boats in existence – and possibly the most beautifully maintained traditional fleet in the world. In fact, in a report on Pengambengan, the Australian National Maritime Museum claimed that these boats could be "the world's most spectacular traditional fishing craft and the largest-scale assemblage of movable cultural heritage in Bali". To see a massed fleet of these vibrant vessels is a privilege that few visitors to Bali would ever expect.

Culturally, this area is almost equally divided between Hindu and Muslim communities, and it is easy to identify the religion of each boat owner: the Muslim boats are frequently decorated with Islamic text and images of holy men, while the Hindu boats often feature a crow's nest in the form of a sacred chariot. It is here that the most important man in the 20-strong crew will sit while at sea; the spotter will frequently earn a share of the takings even bigger than that of the captain. Regardless of religious tendencies, every one of these boats will, prior to launching, have been through complex Madurese ceremonies intended to bring the boat to life ... and further ceremonies are frequently undertaken in the harbour itself to guarantee good hauls of mackerel and sardines.

EAST LOLOAN BUGIS COMMUNITY

15

An unusual collection of stilted houses

Gang Mawar, Loloan Timur, Jembrana

While strolling around the pretty streets of Loloan Timur, near Negara, you'll find it hard to imagine that the hospitable people who welcome you into their family homes are distant descendants of the "Boogie Men" of childhood nightmares: the infamous Bugis pirates who raided the high seas of Indonesia in their stately tall ships. The mythical pirates have long since disappeared, however, and as you wander around there is a very good chance you'll be invited into one of the stilted homes that are of a very unusual design here in Bali. Duck your head as you step through the low doorway. "We're not tall people but Westerners often get headaches in Bugis houses!" your hosts may warn you with a smile.

The Bugis originally came from Sulawesi island (once known as Celebes); nobody is sure anymore when the Bugis community of Loloan Timur was first established, but the villagers will tell you it was well over two centuries ago. There are at least 30 of the traditional Sulawesi-style stilted houses still standing in Loloan, and older people in the community can still communicate in the Bugis language. You will find some of the most beautiful and evocative of these houses down a narrow lane called Gang Mawar ("Rose Alley"), off Jalan Gunung Agung.

There can have been little need for houses to have been built on stilts in this part of Bali, and the open ground-floor utility areas on many of the houses have now been bricked up to create more effective living space. The main supporting pillars of these houses are made from the timber known in Indonesia as *ulin*. In English it is often called Borneo ironwood (*Eusideroxylon zwageri*); it is extremely tough and virtually impervious to termites and rot.

Once inside the house you might notice that it feels a lot like being in the cabin of a ship. This might not be pure coincidence – back in Sulawesi the Bugis have been building traditional timber tall ships, called *phinisi*, for hundreds of years, and their skill as shipwrights has recently been recognised on Unesco's World Heritage List. Their reputation as fearsome pirates arose from tales of six-month-long raiding parties in which they ran their great schooners before the monsoon winds on voyages between their homelands and the distant tribal villages of Papua. They were among the most intrepid sailors in the Indonesian archipelago; you will find Bugis communities on many islands where, perhaps because of their stilted coastal houses, they are often erroneously known as Sea Gypsies. The pretty houses of Gang Mawar, however, are among the most intriguing Bugis communities in the whole country.

KEBUN RAYA JAGATNATHA

16

Homage to what might be our planet's youngest god

Jalan Sudirman, Dauhwaru, Negara, Jembrana

Travellers on the main Denpasar-Gilimanuk highway (which connects with the 24-hour ferry service to Java) are often surprised to see an immense temple entrance – featuring a pair of 8-metre-tall stone suns and a row of five larger-than-life dancing girls. It is particularly fitting that the girls are captured in various poses of the Puspanjali dance – a relatively modern dance that was created in 1989, and is frequently used to welcome honoured guests.

This is the spectacular entrance to Kebun Raya Jagatnatha, a beautifully peaceful garden around which to wander. Nevertheless, unless it is a ceremonial occasion you are unlikely to see another person here, and these gardens remain one of the ignored gems of what is certainly Bali's most overlooked regency capital. While Kebun Raya Jagatnatha is on the route from Java to Bali, it is invariably bypassed by domestic visitors, and you're very unlikely to see Western tourists anywhere in the city of Negara.

As you step through the great solar portals that lead off the main road, you'll find some unexpected architectural formations that seem very different to those in any other temple on the island. On the far side of an expanse of lawns and gardens, you'll see a pair of great swooping black-stone wings, reminiscent of the Garuda, the mythical beast that was the eagle-like steed of the Hindu god Wisnu and, in modern times, a national symbol of the world's biggest Muslim country.

When you walk through this monumental gateway, you'll see a large amphitheatre leading to the entrance to the inner sanctum of the temple (known as the *jeroan*) and it's here that you'll find one of the biggest shrines to Surya (the sun god) on the whole island. Rising to about 20 metres above the temple's inner patio, it is topped with an empty throne and the image of a god that is unique to Balinese Hinduism. The name Sanghyang Widi Wasa dates back to about the 1930s; it refers to an entity that symbolises one almighty god who can then be divided into the Hindu "holy trinity" of Brahma, Siva and Wisnu. This symbol thus conforms to the Indonesian constitutional principal that official religions must be based on a belief in a single omnipotent deity. This spritely looking little figure is always portrayed with flames shooting from his joints. Notoriously hard to define, his other name, Acintya, is often translated as "the inconceivable" or "he who cannot be imagined".

You'll see an image of Sanghyang Widi Wasa adorning the Surya shrine in most temples, yet as a god, he receives no specific offerings, is not followed by any sect or group, and has no temples dedicated specifically to him. From the solar gateways at the front to the massive "sun-god shrine" at the back, Kebun Raya Jagatnatha, however, is about as close as you will come to a temple dedicated to this enigmatic deity.

HARDYS GHOST PLANE ⑰

A Boeing 737 mysteriously abandoned, a five-hour drive from the airport

Jl. Mayor Sugianyar, Dauhwaru, Kec. Jembrana, Kabupaten Jembrana

The Boeing 737 airplane parked atop a grass hillock 2 km north-east of Negara city centre is one of the most unexpected sights you're likely to come across in this part of the Jembrana Regency. Many locals in this area are unaware of the mystery, but local kids talk in hushed tones of the "ghost plane".

The easiest way to find this location is to rely on Google Earth imagery – just look for a white cross standing out clearly amid the greenery of the hills. Although there is, in reality, nothing ghostly about this spot, it is an eerie experience to drive through the usually unmanned security gates at the end of the road and descend to the car park near the plane.

When standing under the wings you'll see that the engine has been removed and it's possible to look straight into the undercarriage chamber, although there is no way to enter the cabin. The green livery on the tail of this Boeing 737-200 would seem to identify it as a defunct part of the Taiwanese EVA Air Corporation fleet.

On the hillside opposite the plane, a newly built (and, it seems, almost immediately abandoned) housing complex gives a possible clue to the idea behind this enigmatic landmark. The land is part of a housing development and timber plantation owned by Hardys Corp. The small residential area remains almost totally abandoned and is, if anything, an even eerier site to explore than the hilltop plane.

According to one of the few local residents, Pak Mura, the plane was transported here in sections a few years ago from Tuban and rebuilt on site. "I don't think Hardys had any plan aside from the fact that they thought it would entice visitors for photo opportunities," he says.

Find more abandoned planes around Bali

This is the least known of several abandoned planes that attract photographers (and selfie addicts) in search of bizarre images from around Bali. One is in a slightly more likely location, 2 kilometres south of the international airport (at Jalan By Pass Ngurah Rai no. 63, Kedonganan, Badung) and has been a fixture of the neighbourhood for more than a decade. Another 737, less accessible, is parked in a quarry near the southern tip of the Bukit Peninsula (on Jalan Raya Nusa Dua Selatan, Kutuh, South Kuta, Badung). It can only be seen either by climbing onto the top of one of the shipping containers that line the road here, or by walking up a short trail onto a treacherously crumbly cliff that overlooks the quarry.

There are vague rumours of optimistic Balinese (or Australian) entrepreneurs who intended to convert these decommissioned aircraft into restaurants, or bars, or villas. For the moment, however, these forlorn flying machines seem destined to remain Bali's mysterious ghost planes.

BATU BELAH

18

The rock broken in two by a fig tree

Dewasana, Pendem, Jembrana

In Balinese philosophy, everything exists in a state of fine balance. Here, in the centre of the world's greatest island nation – on a fiery part of the Ring of Fire – fire and water vie constantly for supremacy, and both elements seem to be given ample representation in the swirling incense and sprinkled holy water of even the smallest everyday ceremony. Even the perennial battle between timber and rock – fought out since the first seedling cracked its way out of an erstwhile barren earth – is a subject for Balinese fascination, and all over the island mighty rock-eating fig trees (called *beringin* in Balinese) are considered sacred.

Six kilometres north of Negara city centre you find a sight that stands as a poignant trophy to the might of wood. Next to a small shrine beside a pretty highland road, a massive egg-shaped boulder – weighing perhaps 5 tons – has been cleaved in half, as if by an axe. The great force that was exerted to do this came from nothing more than a particularly determined fig sapling. Local people will tell you that the rock and the fig tree have been wrestling since before anyone can remember. There's no telling how old the tree might be.

The oldest fig tree in Bali is said to be the weeping fig *(Ficus benjamina)* at Kehen temple in Bangli (see page 202); some experts have estimated that it is well over 700-years-old. Perhaps it's weeping because, unlike the smaller example at Batu Belah, in seven centuries it is yet to split a rock in two.

NEARBY

Puncak Mawar (19)

About a kilometre north of Batu Belah you find the spectacular and delightfully named Puncak Mawar. Rose Peak, as the name translates, is situated at the top of a steep and potholed lane (likely one of the steepest on an island renowned for its near-vertical roads). If you've arrived by car, the best way to reach the peak is to negotiate with someone at the little *warung* on the road opposite Batu Belah; about Rp50,000 will be ample to secure a safe ride to the gravel parking area just a few minutes' walk beneath the peak.

Puncak Mawar offers excellent views across the forests and terraced lowlands around Negara, and across the straits to the jungles of Java's Alas Purwo National Park. The peak has recently been "discovered" by Negara's Instagram generation and a jumble of "selfie spots" have been created – including a cliff-top bicycle, a bamboo bridge-to-nowhere and even a Hobbit Hole.

SACRED HEART OF JESUS CATHOLIC CHURCH

20

The architectural wonder of Bali's Christian heartland

Jalan Dusun Palasari, Ekasari, Melaya, Jembrana
0812 364 6211
Daily 8am–5pm

Out in the west, Bali's "Island of the Gods" nickname takes on more meaning than ever. While the area is largely Muslim, due to immigrants from Java and Madura, and the Hindu villages are vibrantly traditional, the devout Catholic and Protestant communities here date back to colonial times.

West of Negara (Jembrana's provincial capital), you swing off the main road at Blimbingsari and head north for about 3 km. The Sacred Heart of Jesus Church rises above the little village of Palasari, an unexpectedly regal façade against the steaming jungle backdrop.

In other places this incredible building, which was completed in 1958, might qualify as a cathedral, but here it seems so out of place that you might imagine it is some sort of failed missionary-funded tourist attraction. This is far from the truth, however, and the village priest Padre Adi Harun boasts a congregation that would put many churches to shame even in staunchly Catholic countries. "We have about 1,300 Catholics in the village," he says, "and each Sunday at mass we receive between 700 and 800 worshippers."

At Easter and Christmas, crowds swell into the thousands, and the 18 rows of pews under the sweeping Gothic arches are rapidly filled, so plastic chairs are lined up under the shade trees around the church. It might be a Catholic ceremony, but the profusion of traditional *pakaian adat* (traditional Balinese temple attire) and Hindu-style offerings will leave you in no doubt that you're still on the Island of the Gods.

Such accoutrements – along with familiar aspects of Balinese architecture – were part of a deliberate plan by the church leaders (they called it "contextualisation") in which they incorporated local religious aspects to make their ceremonies more accessible to potentially receptive Hindus.

Neighbouring village Blimbingsari has long been a Protestant community (the first Balinese minister was ordained here in 1942), and the Gereja Kristen Protestan is locally known as Pura Gereja – the Church Temple. While it might not match Palasari's Catholic church for sheer audacity, it combines Christian and Hindu architecture in ways that are nothing short of mindboggling: you enter through Balinese *candi bentar* (the split gates that are designed to cleanse the mind) and around an *aling aling* gateway (a blockade against evil spirits) to find a *kulkul* (Balinese warning drum) in place of a church bell, and carved angels with very Balinese features.

BALI STARLING BREEDING CENTRE AT TEGAL BUNDER

21

A secure haven for one of the world's rarest birds

West Bali National Park, Sumber Klampok, Buleleng
Daily 8am–5pm
Prices starts at Rp750,000 for a two-hour trek (it is possible to secure a discount if you just want to visit the breeding centre)

After signing in at the entrance to the West Bali National Park (see following page), the few visitors who make it out here to Bali's far western extreme tend to turn left along the coastal dirt track. If you drive just 200 metres down that lane to the right, however, you're likely to be astounded to come across a barbed wire complex that might seem, if you were in a less peaceful locale, a little like a concentration camp. This heavily protected jungle fortress, complete with electric fences, watchtowers and Kalashnikov-toting guards, is a breeding centre for one of the world's rarest birds, but the staff are keen to welcome visitors (especially if you are happy to donate a little *uang merokok* – "smoking money" – by way of a tip).

The first of these birds recorded for science was collected for Lord Walter Rothschild, and the birds were later named *Leucopsar rothschildi*. It seemed almost to be a case of love-at-first-sight, and the birds' beauty – snowy plumage with black trimmings, a cocky crest and a stunning shock of blue eyeshadow – made them very collec- tible. In the 1970s, hundreds were exported to collectors in the USA and Europe, but few survived long enough to breed in captivity. Starlings are very sociable birds and it is possible that, far from their tropical island territory, they simply died of broken hearts. In 1991 the Jalak Bali (to use its local name) was recognised as Bali's mascot, and an image of the bird was stamped on the face of the 200 rupiah coin. Thus, the bird was elevated to a status symbol in the minds of some of Indonesia's financial elite and became even more collectible.

Less than a century after the bird was first recorded, it was estimated that only five Bali starlings left in the wild; collectors were paying more than US$2,000 for a pair on the black market.

The ranger station at Teluk Brumbun (see page 94) – a boat ride away on the opposite side of the peninsula from Tegal Bunder – is the only place in the world where you can still see wild Bali starlings in their natural habitat. Over 100 have been released on little Nusa Penida island east of Bali, but at Tegal Bunder you can now often see almost 250 of these critically endangered birds flitting through spacious aviaries. The starlings are cared for by a permanent staff of five and protected by seven armed guards while they're prepared for release to boost the wild populations at several similarly armed ranger posts in West Bali National Park.

PRAPAT AGUNG PENINSULA

22

A self-drive safari into the Balinese bush

West Bali National Park, Sumber Klampok, Buleleng
Daily 8am–5pm
Entry fee: Official price-list starts at Rp750,000 for a 2-hour guided jungle-trek (but it is possible to secure a discount if you drive yourself).

Five kilometres east of Gilimanuk, on the Singaraja road, a small turning takes you northwards to the West Bali National Park ranger station. From here, a single rough dirt track leads for about 10 km through the jungle, past Teluk Lumpur (Muddy Bay) to another ranger station, and finally to Pura Prapat Agung, one of the remotest temples on the island.

The track is best avoided in the rainy season but is driveable under normal conditions for most vehicles, if you take it slowly. Very few visitors make the trip all the way out here to Bali's most westerly point – and, perhaps in an effort to increase revenue, park authorities have recently hiked their admission fee substantially. Nevertheless, you can normally get permission to drive your own car into the park.

There's only one road so it is impossible to get lost, but a breakdown could potentially involve either a long, hot hike back out of the forest, or an extremely long wait for another vehicle to pass by.

Out here you'll find it hard to imagine that you're actually on same "crowded" island as Kuta and Nusa Dua. You're sure to see plenty of macaque monkeys (some seem to make an occasional living scrounging from pilgrims who drive through on temple ceremonial days) and the majestic sambar deer known as *menjangan*. Less common sightings are wild pigs (like oversized warthogs), barking deer, muntjac deer, giant monitor lizards, flying foxes and endemic ebony leaf monkeys. Known locally as *monyet hitam* (black monkeys), these beautiful creatures (similar to gibbons or spider monkeys) are sometimes seen looping through the treetops and occasionally scampering on lanky legs across the track. It is said that this sub-species can be found nowhere else in the world.

It will take almost an hour of slow, first-gear rock crawling to reach Pura Prapat Agung temple. The compound is not accessible to visitors, but apart from the novelty of a great coral gateway there is not much to see here. However, on the flat coastal forest just below the temple there is a series of flooded ponds where you can often spot giant monitor lizards and, if you're lucky, pythons.

On the Prapat Agung Peninsula there is a dry, dusty forest that contrasts dramatically with the moist cloud forest that covers the high peaks of the western half of the island. It's a unique wilderness that will give you fresh insight into the diversity of this island.

RANGER STATION AT TELUK BRUMBUN

23

Search for some of the world's rarest birds in their natural habitat

West Bali National Park, Prapat Agung, Buleleng
Open daily
Entry fee; pay at Labuhan Lalang jetty (just off the Gilimanuk to Menjangan road)
Renting a boat to Menjangan Island costs Rp600,000–Rp700,000 if you haggle at Labuhan Lalang, but the trip can be best arranged as part of a snorkelling/ diving tour package (Teluk Brumbun is on the Prapat Agung peninsula, just 200 m from the reefs on Menjangan Island) Camping is possible with a donation to the rangers (around Rp50,000–75,000 per person)

An avian dream of flashing white with dashes of blue eyeshadow, the Bali starling is one of the world's rarest birds. There are several introduced flocks in Bali, but Teluk Brumbun – on the island's remote northwest tip – is the only place in the world where these beautiful and gregarious birds have consistently flown wild. While numbers have plummeted in the past to just five wild starlings, these days you can see more than 20 fluttering and chattering through the trees around the ranger camp of Teluk Brumbun and above the 30-feet-tall aviary that has been built to accommodate new arrivals from the breeding centre at Tegal Bunder (see page 90).

Teluk Brumbun remains almost entirely unknown to even the guides and boatmen who daily shuttle divers and snorkellers from the jetty at Labuhan Lalang to the reefs of Menjangan Island, just 200 metres across the water from Teluk Brumbun. It can easily be included on any trip to Menjangan Island and, while the thrill of being greeted by a wild flock of some of the world's rarest birds is exciting in itself, Teluk Brumbun is also the finest location on the entire island for wildlife watching.

Trek through one of the best areas in Bali for spotting wildlife

A three-hour trek can be organised through the West Bali National Park office at Labuhan Lalang jetty, but even within the immediate surroundings of the Teluk Brumbun ranger station you'll often see Timor deer (known locally as *menjangan*), macaques, rare ebony leaf monkeys, wild pig, civets and giant monitor lizards.

How did the Leucopsar rothschildi *get its scientific name?*

There are conflicting stories. What is certain is that *"rothschildi"* comes from the name of Lord Walter Rothschild, an Englishman born into a banking family. From a young age, Walter was far more interested in the natural world than he was in finance. Some sources say that he captured and named a Bali starling himself, while others say it was captured by ornithologist Erwin Stresemann, who named the bird after Lord Rothschild, his sponsor. It is likely that this second version is correct. According to the Natural History Museum at Tring in the UK (built by Walter's father as a 21st birthday gift to him), Rothschild spent most of his life in the small market town. During his lifetime he employed about 400 collectors and had a collection of 300,000 birds.

BALI SALT

24

Pyramids of salt crystals that make for a unique souvenir from Bali

Jalan Kresna, Pemuteran, Buleleng
Daily 8am–7pm; the factory is closed on Sundays

Down a narrow lane off the main road in Pemuteran there is a small shop that has the power to shape dinner conversations – and flavours – around the world. Lining its shelves is a fascinating array of artisanal sea salts: black charcoal salt; turmeric salt; rosella salt; smoked salt. Some of the wares are fine-grain salts, some are coarse, and others packaged as it formed, in pyramids.

"I don't know how or why the pyramids form, but I just know that they do," says I Made Gelgel, who heads up the business in north Bali. "They usually form a pyramid with a square base, but sometimes, if it's been very dry, then they form a square tile, like a Scrabble piece."

The small salt factory is just down the lane from the Bali Salt shop, and it's well worth a visit – there are no formal tours but ask for Made at the shop and he'll show you around.

The salt comes from the nearby Madurese village of Pejarakan, where for generations people have been making salt by channelling seawater into ponds. The water evaporates under the heat of the sun and leaves behind the mineral-rich salt that is the raw material for Bali Salt.

At the Bali Salt factory – a rather grand term for what is essentially a place where processing is done by hand and by nature – the sea salt is dissolved in freshwater then stored in a tank for a few days. While the water stands, impurities sink to the bottom of the tank. The salty water is then poured into shallow black plastic troughs that stand in a glass "shed" for four days. The shed is heated only by the sun, and temperatures can reach 78 degrees Celcius – stepping inside is like walking into a sauna. It's during the time spent here that salt pyramids grow as the water evaporates.

Once all of the water has evaporated, the salt is removed from the glasshouse and separated by hand into different size granules or pyramids – a worker will sieve the salt, much like panning for gold. Once the sizes are separated, women sift through the salt to remove any remaining impurities, and the salt is then packaged.

The flavours (such as turmeric, rosella and charcoal) are added as the salty freshwater goes into the glasshouse; the smoked salt gets its flavour once the salt is formed, when it's infused for two days with the smoke of coconut husks.

The result is something absolutely delicious – and a very special gift to take home from Bali.

SARCOPHAGI AT PANGKUNG PARUK

25

Last resting place of the first Balinese

Jalan Pangkung Paruk, Pangkung Paruk, Seririt, Buleleng
In Tegallengah, turn off the main Singaraja-Gilimanuk highway into Jalan Yudistira and drive 800m. The site will be on your right-hand side
0812 5288 2110
Open daily
Free, but donations gratefully accepted

Imagine unearthing an ancient treasure chest while ploughing your ric field. That's exactly what happened to a farmer from Pangkung Paruk .. except that he didn't find just one treasure chest, he found four.

The four sarcophagi (ancient stone coffins) had remained undisturbe for around 2,000 years before Pak Wayan went to work one morning i 2014. Incredibly, although they have become a local landmark (anyon you ask can show you where they are), they are still on display in a open *bale* (shelter) next to the farmer's house. In keeping with traditiona Balinese respect for ancestors, they have become sacred relics; offering are regularly made to them, and although you can look and photograp from outside, you may not enter the *bale*.

Nobody is entirely sure of the identity of the people buried in thes stone coffins, but it is safe to say that they were of royal lineage. Tw

bronze mirrors found in the tombs are believed to date back to sometime between 8 and 23 AD. Some of the beads in the sarcophagi are believed to have been produced in India; archaeologists from Cambridge University claim that finds on this part of Bali's coastline suggest established trade routes with India dating back to the first millennium BC. Even more intriguing, in his book *Cultural and Civilisational Links between India and Southeast Asia*, Shyam Saran suggests that the particular style of two beads from a sample of 40 found in the Pangkung Paruk sarcophagi could provide the first evidence of Roman materials in a prehistoric context on a South East Asian island.

It is possible that north-west Bali was a major trading centre around 2,000 years ago. Many of the beads as well as glass, copper, bronze and iron objects found in the graves could not have been produced on the island at that time. About 60 km around the coast west from Pangkung Paruk there was something approaching a prehistoric city at Cekik (near present-day Gilimanuk). More than 100 complete human skeletons, dating from the Neolithic era (as long as 4,000 years ago), were unearthed in a whole series of archaeological digs. The Museum Manusia Purba archaeology museum at the site is open to the public and has some fascinating (and slightly haunting) displays, but there is very little information in English.

It seems that the early Balinese people were inordinately fond of their ani-mals – graves of dogs, horses and chickens have also been found in Cekik. In 1964 a grave was even unearthed that was the last resting place of both a man and his dog.

BALI SEA
Jero Margi
Paken
Singaraja
Lovina Beach
Seririt
Gitgit
Pedawa
S. Saba
Wana Giri
Lake Buyan
Munduk
Lake Tamblingan
Gunung Lesung 1865m
Bedugul
WEST BALI
CENTRAL B

North Bali

0
5 km
10 km
N
s Sari
20
Bondalem
BALI SEA
Madenan
Sambirenteng
Tembok
Mengening
Satra
Batur volcano
outer caldera rim
BALI
21
Sungai kering
Tianyar
Mount Batur
1717m
Kintamani
Lake Batur
EAST BALI
Penelokan
Suter

HYDRANGEA FIELDS OF MUNDUK

①

Where flowers for the god Vishnu are grown

Jalan Kayu Putih–Munduk, Munduk, Buleleng

Bali's history dates back thousands of years, but it's only in the past two or three centuries that the fertile slopes of Munduk in the is-
nd's highlands, shrouded in mist and clouds, have become a productive rming region. Farmers in this cool area, which enjoys average tempera-
ures of 20–25 degrees Celcius, are becoming very prominent producers f blue hydrangea flowers.

According to one legend, the very first people to settle in Munduk ere escaping an invasion of ants. Then, 200 or 300 years ago, several lans resettled here from Klungkung and cleared parts of the forest to rm rice. When the Dutch took control of North Bali and "discovered" Munduk in the late 1800s they cleared the forest further as they esta-
lished plantations of coffee, cocoa, vanilla and cloves, which thrived in e cooler climate at this altitude (500–1,200 metres above sea level).

These days, many of those plantations have been replaced by fields of ydrangeas, which are more lucrative as cash crops, and just happen to e beautiful to look at. Unfortunately, they are also more detrimental to e environment. These flower fields are easy to spot; simply explore the reas around Jalan Kayu Putih–Munduk, between Munduk and Lake amblingan, and look out for vast patches of blue.

Hydrangeas – *pecah seribu* in Indonesian – are a vital component of *anang sari*, the small "trays" made from palm leaves that are filled with etals and placed as offerings in temples, shrines and homes around the land every day.

As with almost everything relating to Bali's Hindu religion, the *canang ri* is charged with symbolism. It relates to the *nawa-sanga*, the complex andala that represents the Balinese universe. The *nawa-sanga* has eight ardinal points and a centre; there are nine gods – eight have a cardinal oint on the mandala, and the ninth has the centre. In the *canang sari* e four main compass points are represented: Visnu, the protector, is in he north and represented by blue petals (usually hydrangea petals); Mahadewa, the great god, is west and yellow; Brahma, the creator, is ed and south; Iswara (a manifestation of Siva) is white and east. The flower" for Siva, the destroyer, is *bunga rampai*, either an assortment of olours or thin slices of pandaan leaves placed in the centre.

There is a lovely sense of continuity when you consider this: today, eople around Munduk are planting hydrangeas so that the blue flowers an be used to visually represent a part of the *nawa-sanga*, but many enerations ago, their ancestors would have been using the *nawa-sanga* determine how they planted their rice crops. This planting method is ill used today – the first nine rice seedlings are planted in a pattern that epresents the *nawa-sanga*.

THE COLONIAL HOUSES OF MUNDUK

2

Retreat homes that trace the development of Indo-Dutch architecture

Jalan Kayu Putih–Munduk, Munduk, Buleleng
The oldest house is about 50 metres down the hill (on the right-hand side) from where Jalan Pura Puseh joins Jalan Kayu Putih–Munduk
0857 3266 0128: Nyoman, a Munduk-based guide

When the Dutch were in control of north Bali, the port town of Singaraja was their base. It was the location of their offices, their seat of power and a lucrative site for trading. But when it came to taking time off, the Dutch headed to the highlands. Lured by the cooler temperatures, forested hills and the tranquil atmosphere, the town of Munduk became their retreat.

While colonial buildings are still prominent in cities like Jakarta, Surabaya and Yogyakarta, in Bali they are rare because the Dutch took control of the island only later in their campaign. Today at least five houses from this era still exist in the village of Munduk. They stand as evidence of the evolution of the Indo-Dutch style of architecture. The Dutch adapted their European sensibilities and Art Deco influences to suit the warmer climes and local building materials; neoclassical columns and thick walls gave way to wood pillars and deeper verandas, longer eaves, larger windows and better ventilation.

The oldest house in Munduk, apparently built in 1890, still belongs to the same family that rented the land to the Dutch. It's a beautiful building that is captivating to explore: the solid, double-thickness walls and neoclassical columns are decorated with hand-carved motifs of Balinese flowers that curve graciously over the shuttered windows. "The wood used in this house is very strong; it's teak," explains guide Nyoman, who has always had an interest in his village's colonial houses. "The wood was carried down from the forests, even though at that time the people believed that tigers lived there."

It's interesting to trace the other colonial buildings in Munduk, which also show the evolution in architectural style: at Pura Sunny Hotel there is a replica of what would have been one of the first Dutch houses to be built in the town; the front room of one private home still boasts geometric Art Deco motifs and a polished concrete floor; and on the oldest building at Guru Ratna Homestay, the veranda filigree is made from wood, not metal. These buildings can be tricky to find, however, and so are best seen with a local guide.

The very centre of Bali

If you ask where the centre of the island is, you're likely to get a variety of responses depending on which part of Bali you're in the time: if you're near Sukawati, for example, someone might say that the Fat Baby statue (see page 174) marks the very centre; if you're in Kintimani, you might be told that it's Pura Pucak Penulisan, the highest temple in Bali. According to the Dutch in the early 1900s, the very centre of Bali was Munduk. And to stake their claim on this, they marked one spot in the town as Kilometre Zero. That marking exists today and can be seen on the road outside the entrance to Puri Sunny Hotel. But the current official Kilometre Zero is Dauh Puri Kangan in Denpasar.

BRAHMA VIHARA ARAMA BUDDHIST TEMPLE

3

A miniature Borobudur and a truly peaceful and spiritual place

Gang Sahadewa, Banjar Tegeha, Buleleng
brahmaviharaarama.com
Daily 9am–6pm (always open for prayer or meditation)

The words Brahma Vihara Arama combine to mean "a place fo self-cultivation". Bali's most beautiful Buddhist temple, just inlan from Seririt on the north coast, is a truly serene spot, offering breath taking views across forested hills, farmland and paddies. From outside the complex appears typically Balinese, with its split *candi bentar* gate guardian statues and three-tiered bell tower. But as Buddha famously said

Peace comes from within. Do not seek it without." So, head inside and you'll find something totally unexpected.

Near the bell tower – which is adorned with an iron bell in place of the usual wooden *kulkul* gong – two sets of stairways, decorated with images of the Buddhist path to enlightenment, ascend towards the main patio and the Panca Bala Stupa. This temple, with its five stupa domes, looks like a miniature version of Java's Unesco-listed Borobudur (a very miniature version – the summit of Borobudur has 72 stupas). The outer walls of this Balinese replica, however, are topped with many more small stupas, along with stone images of Buddha. Under this structure you find a white stone hall (eerily silent), decorated with two sets of murals; one portraying the life of Prince Siddhartha, who became Lord Buddha.

Lotus gardens line the outside of the temple like a spiritual moat. The lotus is a powerful symbol of purity in Buddhism (drip water onto a lotus leaf and you will see how it simply rolls off, like a diamond, without "tainting" the leaf).

Regardless of your religious persuasions, the large patio in front of the main temple is a wonderfully tranquil spot in which to meditate, or to simply ponder in peace. This patio is packed with worshippers on the sixth full moon of each year (around May) for the ceremony to commemorate Vesak, Buddha's birthday. At any time of the year respectful clothing is compulsory (sarongs and sashes can be borrowed from the office).

The temple's founders must have felt that their faith was being tested when, seven days after their new Avalokitaswara Pagoda was inaugurated in July 1976, most of the temple was obliterated in an earthquake that claimed 573 lives. Apparently, head monk Bhante Girirakkhito slept under a table on the patio for the next few months. "Everything created is subject to the law of change," he told his followers. "All things are subject to the laws of nature." So, they set about rebuilding the temple.

In 1982 the Dalai Lama's visit put Brahma Vihara Arama firmly on the spiritual map. A steady stream of Tibetan monks (or those from Myanmar, Thailand, Cambodia, Singapore and other parts of Indonesia) can often be seen passing through the temple following the ritual route of walking meditation. This silent procession can be a profoundly spiritual event to witness.

Vipassana meditation

The temple runs several multi-day Vipassana meditation retreats throughout the year (many held in English) and offers accommodation for participants. Vipassana – which means "to see things as they really are", a clear awareness of what happens as it happens – is a truly profound, ancient meditation technique . The silent sessions are not for everyone (you cannot speak, read or talk for 11 days) but can be very rewarding.

PIONEER MONUMENT IN LOVINA

④

A nod to the founder of "Lovina"

Lovina Beach Hotel, Jalan Seririt–Singaraja, Kaliasem, Buleleng
036 241 005
lovinabeachhotel.com

If you compare a map of Bali drawn 70 years ago with one drawn 30 years ago, what would the difference be? Here's a clue: look at the place names. Another clue? Consider that the letter "v" doesn't exist in either the Balinese or Indonesian languages. Still not sure? Okay, can you spot Lovina on the older map?

The seaside area of Lovina is popular with tourists wanting to head out onto the calm waters in local fishing boats to see dolphins at sunrise. Few travellers, however, would ever know that it was only after the 1950s that the name "Lovina" was used to refer to this area. Nor would they realise that the man who coined that name would be watching after them as they set sail on their dolphin safari.

Just behind the sea-facing gate at Lovina Beach Hotel, there is a concrete statue of Anak Agung Pandji Tisna (1908–1978), a writer and novelist who was also the last king of Buleleng. While holidaying near Mumbai in the early 1950s, Pandji Tisna was quite taken by the relaxing atmosphere and gentle way of life in the coastal areas he visited. He saw parallels between what he experienced there and life in his regency in north Bali, and was inspired to build a seaside resort similar to the one he'd experienced in India.

The initial hotel that Pandji Tisna built in 1953 had only three rooms. He named it "Lovina" – a combination of the English word "love" and the Balinese word "*ina*", which means mother. But many local businessmen were sceptical; it would never succeed, they said. They considered the location – on a beach called Tukad Cebol in Kaliasem village – far too remote to appeal to travellers, and the name too "foreign".

Initially the sceptics were right. Although Pandji Tisna would receive international guests at his Lovina hotel, tourism didn't take off and interest in the area declined after 1958 when the capital was moved from Singaraja to Denpasar. Pandji Tisna's small hotel changed names and he built another hotel 100m away, giving it a Balinese name this time.

Yet somehow the name "Lovina" never disappeared, and by the 1990s it was being used to refer to the string of six beaches that flanked Pandji Tisna's original hotel: Binaria, Kubu Gembong, Hepi, Pemaron, Tukad Cebol and Temukus. These days it is unlikely that travellers would be aware that these other names exist and, as was Anak Agung Pandji Tisna's vision, the name Lovina has become synonymous with the north coast of Bali.

A "Little Museum"

The Lovina Beach Hotel is the site of Anak Agung Pandji Tisna's original three-room resort. Two doors down, in another small hotel also owned by his family, there is a "Little Museum" (according to the sign) that holds the king's typewriter and a few books and magazines from his collection.

BANYUATIS COFFEE FACTORY

⑤

Vintage coffee roasting house

Jalan Raya Seririt–Singaraja, Pemaron, Buleleng
036 224 095
kopibanyuatis.com
Sunday–Friday 8am–4pm; Saturday 8am–1pm

It's often said that "there's no better way to start the day than with a cup of Java". And there are those who claim that Bali has the best coffee in Indonesia. Some sources say that coffee arrived on the island about a century ago from Lombok, though it is believed that Danish trader Mads Lange (see page 36) traded in coffee as far back as the 1840s. If this is true, then he almost certainly would have dealt with Banyuatis Coffee, which claims to be the oldest producer on the island.

According to the company's version of history, in 1800 Jro Dalang Gelgel, a farmer from Banyuatis (on the slopes below Munduk), planted

the first coffee bushes. One hundred and sixty years later, his grandson Ketut Englan opened his roasting house beside the northern coastal road near Singaraja. The roasting process has changed little over the years, and although almost totally overlooked by visitors, this historic roasting plant is a wonderful place for coffee lovers to get an insight into what makes that first cuppa of the morning so special.

Harvesting usually takes place in April and May, but this is just the start of a lengthy process that seems more akin to vintage wine-making – almost three years will pass before the perfected grains land in your cup. The berries are sorted manually, with about 30 per cent being discarded from the top quality selection. The beans are "aged" for two years in a storeroom to make sure they dry out sufficiently. Then they are roasted for exactly 70 minutes over a wood fire. The roasting rooms are pleasantly scented with coffee from huge roasting pans that each hold 200 kg of beans. With a workforce of just 28 people, Banyuatis Coffee produces 60,000 kg of Arabica and Robusta each month.

Kopi luwak: one of the world's most expensive coffees from beans collected from civet droppings

Priced at up to US$1,000/kg, *kopi luwak* is sought after as one of the world's most expensive coffees. The most crucial part of its "brewing" takes place in the digestive system of the civet cat – *luwak* in Indonesian. There's a Thai version that uses elephants and is even more expensive. Banyuatis produces Luwak Arabica coffee, and they claim to use only the beans collected from the droppings of wild civets that live freely on the coffee plantations.

The global reputation this beverage has among connoisseurs stems from the fact that wild civets are extremely finicky eaters and select only the best coffee berries. The drink's popularity, however, has led to the wholesale capture and confinement of "battery civets". Bali Animal Welfare Association (BAWA) has called for a total boycott on *kopi luwak*.

To maximise profits, producers force-feed their timid and terrified nocturnal animals, which are confined until death in tiny wire cages. Countless organised day-trips in Bali include a stop to sample *kopi luwak*. Prices are "irresistible" bargains (compared with Manhattan cafés where you'll pay around US$30 a cup) and tourists are usually shown a couple of civets in tiny chicken wire cages; "These are examples only," the guides will tell you. "The 'working civets' are all happily foraging in the plantations."

You can be sure, however, that you're probably being shown only the healthier inmates of these feline concentration camps.

SINGARAJA'S OLD PORT QUARTER ⑥

Bali's last remaining colonial-era waterfront

Kampong Bugis, Singaraja, Buleleng

The celebrated naturalist Alfred Russel Wallace first landed at the old port area of Singaraja on 13 June 1856. If he returned today, there'd be much that he would recognise, more than 160 years later. Wallace would have registered his arrival at the Customs House; this grand old Dutch building (probably a later version and currently housing the small Museum Soenda Ketjil) still stands on the waterfront near a clutch of stilted *warungs* built on the otherwise disused pier.

The author of *The Malay Archipelago* was hosted in Singaraja by a wealthy Chinese merchant. While the house he lived in has almost certainly disappeared, and the beautiful Chinese temple that now stands on the waterfront would not be founded for another 17 years, much of the area that is still known as Kampong Bugis would have been very familiar. The Chinese community was already dominating trade, and the façades of the shop-houses along Jalan Erlangga are still embossed with the logos of family businesses that dealt in fabrics, traditional cures and even silver and gold that had been worked by Balinese artisans. Even today on Jalan Hasanudin you'll see Chinese *toko obat* (medicine shops) and hardware stores decorated with Chinese lanterns.

"There are about 500 people in the neighbourhood who are descended from the Chinese who arrived up to six generations ago," says Tan Hok Suey, who works as a caretaker in the picturesque Ling Gwan Kiong Chinese temple on the waterfront. "We were here long before the Dutch arrived, and afterwards many other nations also came here to trade."

While the names of Singaraja's inland streets (the Indonesian words for Orange, Mangosteen, Durian, Mango ...) are reminders of the city's agricultural wealth, the names of the streets around the port testify to Singaraja's colourful and adventurous seafaring history: Sumatra Street, Melaka Street, Sumba Street, Sulawesi Street ...

Just 300 metres east of the old port you'll find another Chinese temple called Seng Ho Bio. It is worth exploring this area since the short stroll takes you along Flores Street, through a fascinating and friendly little neighbourhood where fighting cocks and sun-drying fish are more reminiscent of the Sea Gypsy *kampongs* of eastern Indonesia than of anywhere else on Bali.

It's not possible to know for sure, but it's easy to imagine that these are the last relatives of the Bugis people who arrived as sailors from Sulawesi to give their name to the port quarter. In west Bali there is another Bugis community that is well worth a visit (see page 80).

MUSEUM BULELENG

7

A window into all stages of Bali's history

Jalan Veteran 23, Paket Agung, Singaraja, Buleleng
0362 330 3368
Daily 7:30am–3pm

The first thing you're likely to see on your way into Museum Buleleng is the rusting old Fiat that was the official car of I Gusti Ketut Pudja, the first regional governor from 1945 to 1958. It is a reminder of Singaraja's importance in the days when the governor controlled the entire Lesser Sunda Islands, which stretch 1,200 km all the way from Bali through Lombok, Sumbawa, Flores, Sumba and the Alor archipelago to Timor. To put things in perspective, that's a little like the Mayor of London also being responsible for Belgium, the Netherlands, Germany, Switzerland, Austria and the Czech Republic. It's hardly surprising that the old Fiat looks like it's had some wear and tear.

Once powerful, Singaraja (meaning "lion king", from the Sanskrit words *singha* and *raja*) was supplanted as Bali's capital by Denpasar in 1958. The museum, like the sleepy city of 80,500 people, is rarely visited by foreigners. Its exhibits (many from the private collection of the Buleleng royal family) include some items that give a unique insight into the history of this city and Bali as a whole.

The first room contains mostly artwork and brief explanations of characters in the Hindu epics and Balinese mythology. What appears to be a beautiful wooden cabinet in the second room stands as a reminder that even in the material world not all is what it seems. Traditionally known to wealthy merchants here as *brankas* (from the Dutch *brandkast* for "fire-chest"), this is actually a heavy cast-iron safe, made in Austria, cunningly disguised as a wooden cabinet – and according to the plaque, "Garranted Fireproof". It was imported about a century ago by a Chinese trader called Liem Liang An, who had a house near the port.

But it is the collection of ancient artefacts that is most enchanting here. There are droplets of gold that served as early currency, Bronze Age bracelets and sarcophagi that could date back 2,000 years. Found in various parts of Bali, these ancient stone tombs were usually discovered by farmers labouring in their paddies (as were the ones found at Pangkung Paruk, see page 98). They look very much like they could have been measured up for a Hobbit (such as the 60,000-year-old skeleton found in Flores), but apparently ancient belief stipulated burial in the foetal position as the best way to guarantee reincarnation. In Bali, burial sites have been unearthed where jars, as well as stone sarcophagi, were also used as graves.

At Cekik in Gilimanuk, over 100 burial sites have been unearthed, shining light onto the beliefs of the first Balinese people. It's a well-known fact that Bali is home to a colourful and fascinating history, but it's an eye-opener to consider that maybe it stretches back so much further than historians initially thought.

PURI AGUNG SINGARAJA

8

Home of the last king of Buleleng

Jalan Mayor Metra no. 12, Singaraja, Buleleng
081 2392 1658
Daily 9am–5pm

It's not every day that you get to wander unsupervised around the grounds of a royal residence, but that's exactly the privilege you have at Puri Agung Singaraja, the Royal Palace of Singaraja. This unassuming place, once home to the last king of Buleleng, is now a peaceful family residence that pays tribute to the regency's past.

Throughout the courtyard and inside the tranquil buildings are old pieces of furniture, the king's bed, a collection of books, and walls of historic photographs. But don't arrive expecting to see the same style of red brick buildings and elaborate carvings that you find at the palace in Ubud. Puri Agung Singaraja is a "modern" palace that has been shaped by circumstance rather than tradition.

The palaces and independent kingdoms of Bali, which ruled across the island from the early 10th to early 20th centuries, played a very important role in creating the art and culture of Bali that we know today. Eight of Bali's nine current administrative regions (Badung, Bangli, Buleleng, Gianyar, Jembrana, Karangasem, Klungkung and Tabanan) are the former kingdoms that emerged after the powerful Gelgel kingdom broke up in the mid 1600s.

I Gusti Anglurah Pandji Sakti, son of the king of Gelgel, established the kingdom in Buleleng. According to legend, he left Gelgel in Klungkung and upon reaching the peak of a north Bali mountain, plunged his *keris* into the ground. Magically, water began to flow, and to this day a spring still flows from that spot, making it possible for people to live at the top of the hills in Buleleng.

The king chose to settle in Pandji, 5 km southwest of Singaraja. He built three palaces in the vicinity, one of which was in Singaraja, though that *puri* no longer stands. Between 1846 and 1849 there were continuous disputes with the Dutch and eventually, after destroying the palace, the Europeans took control of north Bali in what is now called the Jagaraga War.

The Dutch established their administration in north Bali and nominated a member of the royal family as regent. More than six decades after the first "new" *raja* rebelled against the Dutch, the Europeans appointed his grandson, I Gusti Putu Djlantik, as regent in 1929; it was he who set about building Puri Agung, the palace in Singaraja that you can visit today. Along with the Dutch he also built the nearby Gedong Kirtya, the library of lontar (see pages 158, 160 and 161) in Singaraja. I Gusti Putu Djlantik's son, Anak Agung Pandji Tisna – the founder of Lovina (see page 110) – was the last *raja*, the last king of Buleleng. His children have restored the palace, which had fallen into a state of disrepair, and entry donations are now used to maintain this important piece of Buleleng's history.

SILVER WORKERS OF BERATAN

9

Birthplace of many of Bali's fine art keris daggers

Jalan Mayor Metra no. 83, Beratan, Buleleng
Daily 8am–5pm
Free entry, donations welcome

Follow the main road a couple of kilometres south out of Singaraja centre and you'll find yourself in Beratan village, in a quarter that is marked with the distinctive bright red gates – emblematic of fire – that usually symbolise a neighbourhood of *pande* (the master metalworkers of Bali).

In this case, the *pande* community here is well known for the work they do with silver and gold – in particular, creating religious artefacts such as bells for priests and handles for prized *keris* daggers (see page 196).

In 1856, when the naturalist and explorer Alfred Russel Wallace arrived in Singaraja, the ornate daggers were among the first things he noticed. "We found a number of natives," he wrote in *The Malay Archipelago*, "all conspicuously armed with *kerises*, displaying their large handles of ivory or gold".

Nyoman Suedin's family have been making silver *keris* handles (known as *danganan*) for three generations. Today he works in a tiny workshop in an alleyway just off the main road. "It usually takes me about a month to make one handle," he says, as he taps delicately at the silver with his buffalo-horn hammer. "But if the work is particularly intricate it might take as long as six months."

Beratan remains famous throughout Bali, and priests come to Suedin to buy silver-plated bells and artefacts. Collectors often visit from around the island, and even come across from Java specifically to commission his work.

Many of Suedin's neighbours used to produce top-quality *songket* fabrics (decorated with gold and silver thread). Sadly, these days few people want to splash their budget on a fabric that is replicated by the roll in factories, and Beratan's *songket* industry has almost disappeared. In the old days, the Chinese community in Singaraja were industrious middlemen, selling the *songket* to traders and European travellers. They would import silver, gold and ivory into the island and sell it on as finished artefacts after the *pande* of Beratan had worked their magic on the raw materials.

Many Indonesians subscribe to the spiritual and magical characteristics that are said to dwell in a first-class *keris*. "Beautiful as it might be, a *keris* handle is purely ornamental when it leaves my workshop, Suedin explains. It is up to the buyer to undertake the necessary ceremonies that will breathe life into it and give it the magical qualities he wants."

Thankfully, *keris*-making is still a viable art, since these ceremonial weapons are seen as a status symbol and a valuable heirloom for future generations. The *kusia* handle (emblematic of a curved cocoon) is one of the most popular forms that Suedin produces. It is believed to represent the transformation as the *keris* owner moves to a higher status.

NAGASEPAHA VILLAGE PUPPET MAKERS

(10)

Where colourful characters from the Hindu epics are brought to life

Unnamed road in Desa Nagasepaha, Buleleng
Nagasepaha is about 5 km south-east of Singaraja. Ask in the village for the house of the puppet makers, and you will be directed there.
Open daily, except on Balinese holidays
Free entry, but a donation or small purchase is greatly appreciated

In the small village of Nagasepaha, near Singaraja, one family works tirelessly to produce two of Bali's disappearing traditional arts: they make *wayang kulit* (leather shadow puppets) and intricately detailed glass paintings.

"We have been painting glass and *wayang kulit* for a long, long time," says Gede Kenak Eriada, who first learned the art when he was just eigh

years old. "It's a tradition that has already disappeared from east and west Bali, and now our home is the only place I know of where *wayang kulit* and glass art are created." Gede's home is a bustle of creativity. Five of his family members create the art, and their home is a studio space as well as a showroom.

Wayang kulit is a tradition that has been around for centuries. Translated as "leather puppet", *wayang kulit* refers both to the flat leather puppets that are rear-projected onto a screen, and to the actual performance itself. Typically the *dalang* (puppeteer) tells stories from the Hindu epics, and so the puppets that Gede and his family create are all characters from the epics.

"When we paint on glass we can express ourselves, but when we make *wayang kulit* we cannot have our own style. They must all be made the same," explains Gede. "In Java, the puppets are bigger than ours, and here we use more colours. Different areas have different styles, but we must keep our area's style."

The puppets are made from cowhide that Gede's family buys "fresh". They then stretch it and leave it to dry for five days before the creative work begins. The puppet will be cut (both its physical shape and the holes that give the shadow puppets their details), painted and finally the limbs will be attached to the body. Even though an audience will not see the colours of the puppets during a performance, they are very carefully detailed and painted so that the *dalang* can tell the characters apart.

"To make one *wayang kulit* it will take 15 to 20 days, and the most expensive one we sell costs Rp3,500,000; the cheapest is Rp300,000," says Gede. "It is a lot more difficult to make the puppets than it is to paint on glass. It will take you months to learn the reverse glass painting, but to make the *wayang kulit* you need to learn for years."

Glass painting, a relatively new art form in Bali that is thought to date back to about 1910, has a link to *wayang kulit*; the paintings also tell stories from the Hindu epics. The painting, which will take between seven and 10 days to complete, is done in reverse on the back of the glass.

Most of the glass paintings Gede's family produces are commissions for family homes (where they will be placed in shrines), while the *wayang kulit* will either be used in performances or as decoration. "If you play with the puppets they will break sooner, but they could last decades," says Gede.

In 2003 Unesco designated *wayang kulit* as one of the Masterpieces of the Oral and Intangible Heritage of Humanity. In his book *A House in Bali*, composer Colin McPhee tells beautiful stories about watching and listening to *wayang kulit* performances that lasted many, many hours – often through the night and into the early hours of the morning.

JEMBONG WATERFALL

11

A veil of water with healing properties

Follow the signs from Ambengan village, Buleleng
Ticket office open 7am–7pm

The roads leading to Ambengan village are perfumed with the scent of cloves – it's a magical introduction to a waterfall that the Balinese say has special healing powers. The road also offers a wonderfully relaxing approach through plantations and farmlands where people are still very connected to the earth and seasons. Life here seems to happen at a natural, gentle pace.

For the time being this waterfall, which creates a wide veil as it cascades down steps of rocks, is very much off the radar. But it probably won't be for long. As with many places in Indonesia, the government has stepped in and tried to manufacture a "tourist attraction" from what is a naturally beautiful site. Just above where the cascading water meets the village, there are now two pleasant man-made swimming pools that channel water from Jembong. Above them, a zipline waits for thrill-seekers. There are selfie spots too: on stepping stones in a little pond, and on a bridge that crosses in front of the falls.

Despite the obvious human intervention, Jembong is a lovely place to cool off or to use as a starting point for a hike through what's been called the "Secret Garden of Sembangan" to the well-known Aling Aling waterfall. You can arrange a guide for this at the ticket desk.

The new concrete road from Ambengan to Jembong's car park is wide enough for one car only, and it criss-crosses with the channelled water from Jembong. Once you arrive in the car park you can see the falls, but you will need to climb a few steps to reach the pools, and a few more to reach the base of the falls.

SEKUMPUL WATERFALL

⑫

A waterfall to inspire the creators of Jurassic Park

Follow the signs from Pura Desa Sekumpul, Sekumpul, Buleleng
Ticket office open 7am–5pm

Beautiful, majestic, magical, breath-taking, spectacular: when you undertake any online research on Bali's natural attractions you'll find a string of similar adjectives used to describe the island's many waterfalls. You'll also find a plethora of lists covering "the top five most dazzling waterfalls on Bali", "Bali's most enchanting waterfalls", "the 10 most awe-inspiring waterfalls in Bali" ... and often these lists cover the same handful of waterfalls that have become favourites for those who document their travels on Instagram. But there is one waterfall that, for now, has escaped most of the lists: Sekumpul.

With an average annual rainfall of 1,715mm and a chain of volcanic mountains running east to west towards its north coast, you can be certain that Bali has an abundance of waterfalls. Most tend to be on the northern side of the mountains where the land is fairly steep, and the popularity of the waterfalls usually depends on their location and accessibility. Sekumpul is just far enough off the beaten track to keep visitor numbers down.

Sekumpul means "get together" in Indonesian, and what makes this waterfall special is that it's actually a group of up to seven waterfalls within a few hundred metres of each other, depending on the time of year (there are more during rainy season, which is from October to April). Also, after it rains, the main waterfall becomes a two-coloured cascade; water on the left comes from a spring near the top of the cliff and remains clean, while the water on the right runs as a stream through villages and paddies, picking up silt that turns it brown.

The setting of Sekumpul is truly beautiful: water seems to ooze its way through the jungle, cascading between trees, moss and ferns to the pools about 80 metres below. During the wet season it can be difficult to separate some of the waterfalls, as water fans out across pretty moss-covered rock faces from under and between jungle vegetation.

The walk down to the base of the main waterfall will take around half an hour. The trail, which will be slippery when wet, is well maintained and consists of a concrete path, concrete steps and a sturdy industrial-style metal staircase that leads down a cliff face. While having a guide (Rp250,000 for two people) is not necessary as the path is obvious, it's likely that, when you pay your entrance fee, people from Sekumpul village will insist that you take one with you. You can try to resist, but do keep in mind that you'll be supporting the local community and that the guides help to keep the area clean by picking up litter along the way.

NATURAL PALM SUGAR PRODUCTION

(13)

A traditional cottage industry where palm sugar is produced

Banjar Dinas Singkung, Sudaji, Sawan, Buleleng
Open daily
Family home; no charge but donations appreciated

Kadek Kamiarsa, who learned how to make palm sugar from his grandfather, is the latest in a long line that dates back more generations than the family can remember. At the family home (which is down a narrow motorbike track deep in the forested valley of the Sudaji River), the production of palm sugar from the little plantation of aren trees (*Arenga pinnata*) has changed little over the centuries.

The simplest possible ladder – known locally as a *bangul*, a thick bamboo pole notched at every section with a toe hole – is used to climb the tree to collect the liquid that becomes palm sugar. When a thick shoot starts to form where the flowers grow off the main trunk (this is where the liquid comes from) it must be hammered every day for five days with a heavy wooden mallet called a *palu*.

"This is supposed to get the sap flowing," Kamiarsa explains. "Even so, it is a bit of a gamble; it will take about another 10 days for the flowers to turn black and that's when we start tapping the sap. The trouble is, you really can't tell until you start, and sometimes, for no apparent reason, the tree is dry and you have to start again."

If, however, the sap is running as it should, then as much as 4 litres per day can be tapped from a single tree. This liquid (known as *tuak*) tastes like sweet, slightly musty lemonade and is deliciously refreshing when chilled. At this stage *tuak* is still non-alcoholic, but in many places, coconut husk and bark from a tree that the Balinese call *kutat* are added for flavour, and after a further five days of fermenting it is possible to produce an alcoholic drink that might be as strong as 20 per cent by volume (see page 162).

But at Kamiarsa's family home the end product is refined *gula merah* (literally "red sugar"). "We collect the sap from the trees every morning and afternoon," says Kamiarsa. "We boil it for up to five hours – blowing through a bamboo tube called a *semprong* to keep the fire hot – until just the thick brown residue is left. This is the sugar."

Kamiarsa's family recipe includes the use of leaves from a tree called *kayu apit*. The leaves boil away entirely during the process and stop the sugar from becoming too dark in colour. The liquid palm sugar is then poured into half coconut shells to solidify. Each shell has a hole drilled in the bottom to allow the semi-circle of palm sugar to fall out easier. These domes of natural sugar are then sold at the local market.

The finished sugar is so flavoursome that it can be eaten raw as a sort of natural fudge. Experts claim it contains iron, zinc, calcium and potassium. By comparison, refined white table sugar is nothing but empty calories.

SURYA NADA GONG WORKSHOP ⑭

A workshop where traditional Balinese gongs are produced

Kawanan village, Sawan, Buleleng
0878 6161 2908
Daily 8am–5pm
No charge, donations gratefully accepted

Gongs are often prized as heirlooms and ancient trade items all over Indonesia, but they are rarely as important as they are in Bali, where they are the central instruments in the island's ubiquitous *gamelan* music (see page 14). Gongs come in a variety of sizes and are designed by master bronze-workers so that they resonate at the perfect pitch. The biggest of the gongs used in Balinese *gamelan* is known as *gong wadon* and is suspended vertically when played. It can be almost a metre in circumference.

"To make a gong like that, we work in a team of four men," says gong-maker Made Suanda. "One person turns the bronze plate and three others hammer it."

The bronze is smelted at 800 degrees for three hours in a stone-floored workshop where smoke and sparks swirl, like an alchemist's laboratory. It's a fitting analogy, since Suanda's family has been turning out magical instruments at the Surya Nada Gong Workshop for four generations.

Racks of smaller gongs, played horizontally, are known as *trompong*. "It might take us six or seven months to make a full *trompong* set of 12 pieces," says Suanda. "And a single 3 kg gong might fetch about US$180."

The raw material used to make gongs at Surya Nada is almost exclusively shards of bronze from broken gongs that are shipped to Bali from Java. Eventually a gong will crack; it is then bought by middlemen who sell the pieces by weight. Suanda currently buys from them at around US$15 per kilogram of bronze.

In many parts of Indonesia, especially Kalimantan, old gongs are prized family heirlooms that are believed to house spirits. As modern material possessions become more important and traditional beliefs lose traction, many households can be convinced to sell such items to middlemen, since even a relatively small gong will contain about 3 kg of bronze. Some of these gongs will be highly valuable, such as the Indonesian gong on display in London's British Museum that was part of the collection of Sir Stamford Raffles and is believed to have been made in the 1750s. The middlemen will reap the benefits from such finds. Others are simply venerable pieces of family history that are likely to be chopped to jagged shards and end up on the *landasan* (anvil) in gong foundries like Surya Nada.

In Bali, blacksmiths are known as *pande* (similar to a caste), but this is far more than simply an occupation, someone born into a *pande* family will always be known as a *pande*.

As with any Balinese workplace, Suanda's workshop has a place of honour reserved for the traditional shrine. But in this case, rather than being painted the usual yellow, the *pande* shrine is red, revered as the colour of fire.

SULING WORKSHOP IN SAWAN

⑮

Where the sounds of Bali are made

Desa Sawan, Banjar Asem
Near Pura Alit Manik Sari, which is near the statue in the road in Sawan
Ask for the home of Made Suete

The hypnotic sounds of *gamelan* music can be heard all over the island: from the arrivals hall at Ngurah Rai International Airport to shops, cafés, homes and village streets. *Gamelan* music (see page 14) is an integral part of life in Bali. It is "a kaleidoscope of sound and rhythm that is reco- gnised today as one of the world's most sophisticated musical traditions" says Michael Tenzer, assistant professor of Music at Yale University and a recognised authority on Balinese *gamelan*. But where do the instruments come from?

Little Sawan in north Bali is known to be one of the villages where gamelan instruments are made. And in this village, a man named Made Suete is said to be one of the best makers of *suling* (bamboo flutes) on the island. Almost anyone in the village will be able to direct you to his house, where you can watch him crafting his instruments; it's a fascinating process to witness.

A *suling* is a simple-looking bamboo flute, and in each gamelan ensemble there are likely to be at least eight of the instruments, which give a very expressive sound to the musical arrangement. "There might be four bigger *suling*, and four smaller ones," says Made Suete, a fourth-generation gamelan maker. "The music in different areas has a different sound, and so while you also get *suling* in Java, in Bali they are used differently."

The instruments can be various sizes: the smaller *suling* (around 20 cm in length) give a higher-pitched sound and are more common as they're easier to play, while the large ones (up to a metre in length) need to be rested on the ground when played. "Many people will play the *suling*, but it is rare for someone to be able to play one properly," explains Made Suete. "You have to breathe in a special circular way and always keep your cheeks filled with air."

Made Suete makes creating *gamelan* instruments look so simple; while working on one called a *rindik* – like an upside-down xylophone – he hits a piece of dry bamboo with a piece of rubber cut from an old tyre then shaves it with a knife to change its sound. The correct sound, the correct pitch, is carried in his head; he tunes the instruments by ear. For this reason, he says, it "is better if one person makes all the instruments. A *gamelan* is like a family."

BENGKALA VILLAGE OF THE DEAF

16

A village with a language found nowhere else on Earth

Bengkala, Kubutambahan, Buleleng

Kolok Pinda steps up to the *warung* counter and silently orders a coffee, wiggling his finger against his forehead in the same way that Westerners would imply somebody is slightly crazy ... or perhaps someone who is in the throes of a caffeine buzz. The woman who serves him replies to his signalled thanks by sliding her left hand off her right palm as if a slate is being wiped clean.

Kolok Pinda is one of 42 deaf people in Bengkala village – the only people in the world who use this unique local sign language, known as Kata Kolok, as their first language. The woman who served his coffee is not hard of hearing, but more than half of the villagers in Bengkala are at least proficient in this dialect.

Local people claim that a single deaf woman was the original source of the "epidemic" about seven generations ago, but in surrounding villages people will often simply shrug and announce that it was the outcome of "some kind of curse". Recent scientific research, however, has shown that the deafness is caused by a recessive gene in this once isolated

community, where as many as one in every 50 people in the village are born deaf.

While deaf people in the village are distinguished by having the word *kolok* ("deaf" in Balinese) in front of their name, they are integrated into local life to a level rarely seen elsewhere. Rather than marginalising the *kolok* individuals and families, more than half of the entire village is able to communicate using a language found nowhere else on Earth. *Kolok* men here play an active and valid part in community meetings outside of the village, with the help of friends who voluntarily translate for them. There are many cases of marriages between hearing and non-hearing partners in which the common language for the family is Kata Kolok. In some ways it often appears to be more normal to be deaf in Bengkala; some classes in the village school are even given, for all pupils, in sign language.

Kata Kolok is perhaps as widely used now as it ever was, and locals in the village enjoy teaching visitors the basics of their unique language. Many of the signs are delightfully descriptive: fingers curled into hook-shaped fangs symbolising a dog; a gentle preening motion denotes a cat; and the symbols for male and female are unmistakable in their resemblance to genitalia.

A troupe of traditional dancers, nine of whom are deaf, have become so well known in the area that they occasionally dance at cultural performances in other villages with their unique Janger Kolok (Dance of the Deaf, see page 137).

KEM WEAVING

⑰

Exquisite textiles woven by Bengkala's kolok women

Unnamed road; follow the signs from the main road that leads into Bengkala, Buleleng
For dance performances contact Ketut Kanta: 0812 3748 4230
Daily 8am–5pm

The village of Bengkala (see page 134) is a special place. Due to a recessive gene, a relatively high percentage of people in this once isolated village are born deaf, and more than half of the village's community can

ommunicate though a unique sign language that has developed over the ast seven generations. Within the village, the deaf people – referred to s *kolok* – are an integral part of the community, however they do tend to e among the poorer community members.

The *kolok* men have a reputation for being strong and fearless, and hey tend to get work doing manual labour in the fields, monitoring the idge-top community's water pipelines and digging graves. Like the vilage's hearing women, the *kolok* women's time is usually spent working at ome and they don't have much opportunity to earn a living. There is one lace, however, where a handful of *kolok* women earn an income.

KEM is a community centre on the outskirts of Bengkala, and it's here hat *kolok* women weave exquisite textiles. KEM, which stands for Kawasan Ekonomi Masyarakat ("Community Economic Area"), was set up by state-owned oil company Pertamina; often the fabric woven at KEM is used for the uniforms of Pertamina employees. Sarong fabric is also woven and sold to the few tourists who pop in to this lovely centre.

"I am so happy to weave here because before I wasn't able to earn money," signs Kolok Budewati, one of the deaf women who has been weaving at KEM for the past few years. In the village the word *kolok* always precedes a deaf person's name.

Making one sarong is a time-consuming process. If there are no ceremonies in the village it will take six straight days to weave a single 3-metre-long sarong. "But that's not what takes the most time," says Ibu Sami, a hearing woman whose husband and father-in-law are deaf, and who oversees the weaving centre. "It will take two of us 20 days to set up one loom." That set-up will last about six months, during which time the weaver will make about 40 sarongs with thread bought from a supplier in Singaraja.

Janger Kolok: a special dance performed by deaf dancers

While KEM is on the premises of Ibu Sami's family home, it is also a kind of community centre for the *kolok*, who gather there regularly to practise their dancing. Janger Kolok is a special dance performed by some of the *kolok* in Bengkala, and they sometimes perform at events around the island.

Another reason to visit KEM is to buy the *jamu*, a traditional turmeric-based drink that is also produced by Ibu Sami and the *kolok* women at KEM. They've called their drink Sakuntala (derived from the words *suri*, *kunyit*, and Bengkala); it sells for Rp6,000 per small bottle.

DRAGONFRUIT PLANTATIONS NEAR BULIAN

(18)

Forests of cacti that bear remarkable fruit

South-east of Singaraja, close to Bulian, Buleleng

f you head east out of Singaraja towards Air Sanih and take any one of the roads to the south, you'll find yourself crossing narrow valleys and avelling on steep, picturesque roads as you make your way towards Bali's ınd of dragons.

Reaching an elevation of around 2,000 metres, the island's central ighlands are not the highest peaks on Bali – the mighty Mount Agung, hich reaches a height of 3,031 metres, lays claim to that – but it's not on ie peaks that the dragons dwell. Instead, you'll find them on the lower orth-facing slopes. Up here, in the rain shadow of the central highlands, he fertile volcanic soils and drier climate provide everything the dragons eed to thrive, and at certain times of the year you'll see them in their housands as flashes of delicate white flowers erupt into the vibrant deep ink flames of *buah naga* – dragonfruit.

Originally from Costa Rica and Nicaragua, where the *Hylocereus cos-aricensis* is called *pitahaya*, the pink fleshy fruit is known around Asia as ragonfruit, which is as likely a reference to the scale-like shape of the ruit's skin as it is to the almost red colour, and the fact that it resembles ames shooting out of a dragon's mouth.

The slopes close to Bulian village are where the majority of *buah naga* re grown in Bali, and they really are an unusual sight. While you might ome across one or two of the cacti growing against a fence post in villages round the island, up here the vine-like cacti have been planted row upon ow upon row, one cactus to one post. The plants grow up to about 1.5 netres then cascade over the scooter tyre "garters" that support each one

The hardy cacti have no leaves; the fleshy stems (through which pho-osynthesis happens) have three ribs ridged with little clusters of short pines. The fragile-looking flowers are remarkable. Buds that look like a ollection of lime-green tendrils fold back at night to reveal a flower with ery long, delicate white petals. The fruit of course grow from the flower, ınd there are said to be about seven "flushes" of flowers per season.

The Costa Rica nightblooming cactus, as the plant is also known, is relatively new addition to the agricultural sector in Bali. While today ou'll find the vibrant pink fruit on the menu of almost every trendy afé from Canggu to Ubud, two decades ago you probably wouldn't have ound them on the island at all. Many older Balinese people still refuse to at the fruit. "It's new, we don't trust it," they say.

To many travellers, dragonfruit is as exotic and mystical a fruit as you ould hope to find. The flesh of the bright, deep pink fruit is peppered with tiny seeds – much like a kiwifruit and similar in texture – and it has perfectly balanced sweet-yet-earthy flavour. Cafés and restaurants serve dragonfruit aplenty in Bali; as well as adding a very Instagrammable factor o a dish, the fruit is packed with antioxidants and vitamin C.

TRADITIONAL BAMBOO RAFTS

(1

A bamboo boat tradition that could predate modern humans

Kubutambahan (10 km east of Singaraja), Buleleng

The first known sea voyage in history took place from Bali to Lombok around 850,000 years ago. While *Homo erectus* could have populated ali via land bridges, it's the stone tools found on Flores island that have led storians to the conclusion that he must have built bamboo rafts to cross e intervening straits.

Near Bali's northernmost tip, Tanjung Bungkulen, fishermen are con- ructing great 8-metre-long bamboo rafts even today. But these are not cean-going boats meant for voyages of exploration as in days of old. These fts (known as *rompong*) are part of an ancient fisheries industry that still ırvives in many parts of Indonesia.

"It takes us about a week to make a raft," the fishermen explain. "The amboo comes from valleys at the foothills of the volcanoes. These days we se plastic drums to add to flotation and plastic twine, which is now easier find than rattan, but apart from that, everything we use is natural."

Only a couple of these *rompong* rafts are likely to be under construction any one time on the beach near Kubutambahan fishing village, but the each here (very rarely visited by tourists) is also fascinating for the countless utrigger fishing boats known as *jukung* (see page 64).

Motorised *jukung* are used to tow the bamboo rafts out to sea, where ıey act as floating islands that attract schools of fish. A small hut might e built on the deck to shelter a worker whose job it is to light the lamps ıat will attract fish at night. In what must be one of the world's loneliest bs, a boatman might be stationed on a *rompong* anchored to the seabed ıore than 100 km off the coast; he will be visited each week by a boat that rings supplies and collects the catch. In September 2018 an Indonesian eenager was rescued near Guam island (almost 3,000 km from his home), truggling to survive in open ocean seven weeks after his *rompong* broke its nchor rope in a storm.

In 1990 Charles Zerner (a consultant for the World Resources Institute n Washington) estimated that more than 200 *rompong* were operating in he Madjene area of Sulawesi in an increasingly competitive industry; the ishing teams likened their floating rafts to gardens where they could harvest rops of mackerel and tuna. Zerner reported that traditional laws stated that afts should not be anchored less than 3–5 km from each other (i.e. within ight), and that crews had the right to destroy a rogue raft that had come oose from its anchor to imperil neighbouring *rompong*.

The Kubutambahan fishermen claim that (although not visible from and) there are as many as 50 of these *rompong* rafts anchored about 20 km ffshore. If such numbers are true, then competition is rife on the open seas ff Bali's north coast.

JULAH VILLAGE

(2

Where history is recorded on a guarded treasure

Jalan Pura Desa, off Jalan Airsanih-Tejakula, Julah, Tejakula, Buleleng
Note that Julah is incorrectly indicated on Google Maps; the village is situated 29 km east of Singaraja on Jalan Airsanih-Tejakula

The little *warungs* and shops that line the main road of Julah, 29 k east of Singaraja, might fool you into thinking Julah is just a regul Balinese village. It is, in fact, steeped in a history that dates back more tha 1,000 years.

Julah is the sister village of Sembiran, which is further inland, and was there that the "Sembiran inscriptions" were spotted in 1890 by J. H Liefrinck, the Dutch Controleur of Bali (at that time the villagers didn realise that the sacred icons were in fact inscriptions.) These inscriptions

rasasti in Indonesian – are royal edicts inscribed on 20 copper plates that ate to between 951 AD and 1181 AD. Archaeologists say they were issued y six different kings over a 200-year period and were addressed directly to e people of Julah. Written in Old Javanese, Old Balinese, and with some anskrit words, the *prasasti* cover 200 years of the village's history.

Although you'd never suspect it today, Julah was a major port village uring the 10th and 11th centuries; Spice Route traders and plundering irates were frequent visitors. According to the inscriptions, there were nany social conflicts over the years, and one of the plates (dating back to 016 AD) states that only 50 of 300 families survived one attack by pirates.

The plates have had their share of conflict too (they were stolen, but ecovered in Java before they left the country), and these days it's unlikely ou'll get to see the plates. Half are now kept in Sembiran and the other alf in Julah, their locations a closely guarded secret.

"These copperplate inscriptions are venerated as sacred heirlooms," vrote German anthropologist Dr. Brigitta Hauser-Schäublin in her 012 academic paper *The diversion of the village gods: A criminal turn in he biography of Balinese copperplate inscriptions*. "They are referred to as *ratima* (sacred material representations of gods) and addressed as Ida Bhatara (deified ancestors or gods) who have a distinct agency. They are aken out of their hiding places and ritually cleansed by senior members of the *kerama desa* during temple festivals when they are worshipped."

It is said that the Sembiran inscriptions were once kept in Julah's Bale Agung temple. This old temple lacks the ornate sculptures and murals hat are so iconic of Balinese Hindu temples, and apparently dates back to he late 9th or early 10th century. "We know the age because of the original Cakra symbols that remain on the wooden door in the temple," says Ketut Sideman, caretaker of Pura Bale Agung.

It is worth stopping off in Julah to see Pura Bale Agung and the magni-ficent banyan trees at its entrance. Unlike most temples on the island, one may not enter the temple – "Julah's village temple may only be entered after its ritual opening just before a temple festival starts," notes Hauser-Schäublin. "To set foot in the temple without a ritual occasion represents a pollution of the temple." It is possible to walk around the temple, however, and by just looking over its walls (which stand about chest high) even a casual observer will notice that this temple is architecturally distinct from almost any other on the island.

To learn more about the fascinating history and stories of Sembiran and Julah, read *Burials, Texts and Rituals – Ethnoarchaeological Investigations in North Bali, Indonesia*, edited by Brigitta Hauser-Schäublin and I Wayan Ardika. It is available as a free download.

PURA DALEM BALINGKANG

A Chinese Buddhist temple within a Hindu temple, symbolising the union of two cultures

Pinggin, Kintamani, Bangli
Always open, but a sarong is required to enter

High up in the hills there is a temple that stands as a reminder of a love that spanned cultures and religions. That temple is Pura Dalem Balingkang in the village of Pinggan, directly north of Mount Batur's peak. There are many components to the Hindu temple, but if you follow the steps up, walk along a pathway to the main section of Pura Dalem Balingkang and turn to your right, close to the temple's *kulkul* you'll see a Chinese Buddhist temple decorated with lanterns and a large red Chinese coin carved into the outside wall.

There is no way now of separating fact from fiction, and there are various versions of the story that explain the history and reasons behind this temple. Pura Dalem Banlingkang dates back to the 12th century, to when Raja Sri Haji Jayapangus was a king in north Bali. According to one version of the story, while walking in a market one day the king came across a beautiful woman named Kang Ching Wei, the daughter of a wealthy Chinese merchant. He fell instantly in love with her and they married. When the king built the temple he named it Balingkang – an amalgamation of the words Bali and Kang – in honour of his wife and as a symbolic union of the two cultures. It is highly likely that this wedding is where the tradition of using Chinese coins in Hindu offerings began (see page 20).

Raja Sri Haji Jayapangus and Kang Ching Wei are still celebrated today. As part of a ceremony called Barong Landung, enormous effigies of a dark-skinned king and a light-skinned queen are carried through the streets of Pinggin. According to one legend, these effigies had a sinister origin ...

Even after years of marriage, Raja Sri Haji Jayapangus and Kang Ching Wei had no children. This worried the king, who went to Mount Batur to meditate. While there he met a woman named Dewi Danu; he didn't mention that he was already married and they ended up having a son together. Eventually Kang Ching Wei went in search of her husband. She found him living with Dewi Danu, who was shocked to discover that Raja Sri Haji Jayapangus was already married. In a fit of rage Dewi Danu's mother used her magical powers to burn the king and Kang Ching Wei. The king's subjects went into mourning and built two effigies in honour of their king and queen. It is these effigies that are replicated today.

While it's likely that the stories behind this temple have been muddied by time, the symbolism of the mixed cultures and religion is indicative of Bali today; people of different religions live peacefully side by side. Indonesia is the largest Muslim country on earth, home to 13 per cent of the planet's Muslim population, yet only 13 per cent of Bali's population are Muslim. Almost 84 per cent of Balinese people are Hindu, 2.5 per cent are Christian and only 0.5 per cent are Buddhist.

Kintamani dogs: Indonesia's only dog breed

As you travel up into the highlands of Bali, around Kintamani (Bangli), you may notice that as you get higher, many of the dogs tend to look less like the typical Bali street dogs and a lot more like miniature Alaskan malamutes. What you're looking at will likely be Bali's very own breed of dog: the Kintamani.

The dogs, which are most often white but can also be black or brindle, are also known by their nickname, "Kinta". They stand about half a metre tall, with a medium-length coat, a fluffy curved tail and soft, thick ears that always look alert.

"These dogs are excellent hunters," says Pak Ketut Lingga, as his three dogs (Pony, Bibit and Bobby) sit diligently outside his house in a small village near Kintamani. "They are also very clever and loyal, and are known to be good guard dogs." Kintas also have an excellent sense of smell and there are reports of them being used as sniffer dogs by the National Narcotics Board of the Republic of Indonesia.

The origin of these dogs isn't known, although according to folklore, the breed originated about 800 years ago. The story goes that when a wealthy Chinese man named Lee moved to the Kintamani region and married into the family of King Jayapangus (see page 144), he brought a Chow Chow with him and the Kintamani breed evolved from that dog.

Science has proven this myth wrong, however. In a 2005 study of the dogs' genetic profile published in *The Journal of Heredity*, researchers note that their findings "confirm that the Kintamani dog was derived from the local feral Bali street dogs and not the Chow Chow ... The even closer relationship of the Kintamani and Bali street dogs to Australian dingoes was significant and thus supports the theory that Australian dingoes originated from dogs of East Asia that followed human Austronesian expansion into the islands of South East Asia." Both the Kintamani and Bali street dogs tend to whelp in burrows, which, the researchers say, is a trait of wild dogs.

Kintamani dogs are rarely found outside of Bali, but they are recognised as a breed by many kennel clubs around the world. Efforts are underway to have the dog accepted as a recognised breed by the Federation Cynologique Internationale (the largest international federation of kennel clubs in the world).

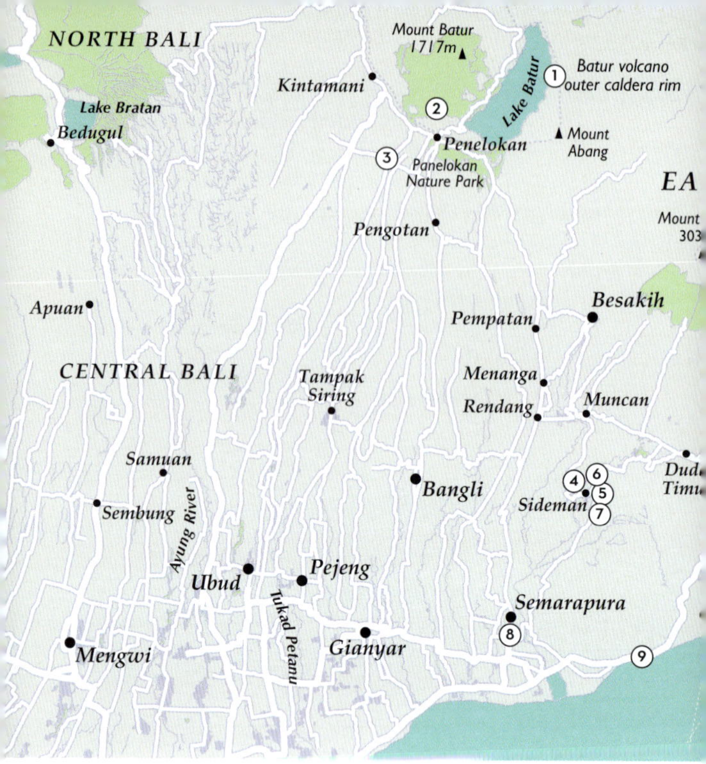
NORTH BALI
Mount Batur
1717m
Kintamani
Lake Bratan
Bedugul
Lake Batur
Batur volcano
outer caldera rim
Penelokan
Mount
Abang
Panelokan
Nature Park
EA
Mount
303
Pengotan
Apuan
Besakih
Pempatan
CENTRAL BALI
Tampak
Siring
Menanga
Rendang
Muncan
Samuan
Bangli
Dud
Timu
Sembung
Ayung River
Sideman
Ubud
Pejeng
Tukad Petanu
Semarapura
Mengwi
Gianyar

East Bali

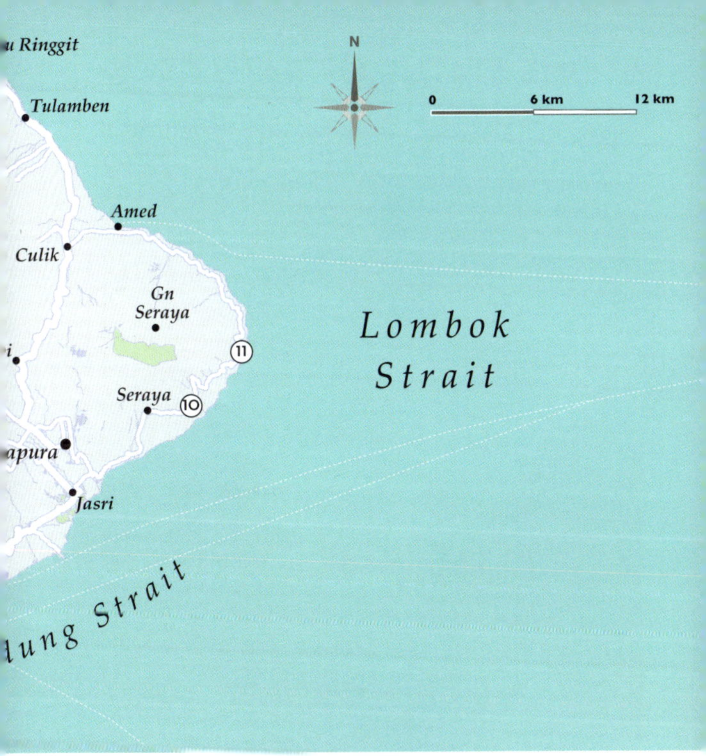
u Ringgit
N
0
6 km
12 km
Tulamben
Amed
Culik
Gn
Seraya
Lombok
Strait
11
Seraya
10
apura
Jasri
lung Strait

STONE STATUE OF RATU GEDE

①

Home of Trunyan's "unspeakable" treasures

Pura Pancer Jagat Trunyan, Trunyan, Kintamani, Bangli
The temple is officially closed to the public but access may be granted on polite request if you are wearing a sarong
Free entry, but donations gratefully accepted

The spectacular Batur crater lake has a circumference of about 22 km. At the remotest extreme on its eastern shore you'll find Trunyan, a Bali Aga – some say the "original" Balinese – village (see page 212).

The true fascination with Trunyan lies in the things you *cannot* see or even speak of. Pura Pancer Jagat Trunyan (the main temple) is the location for a secret artefact that few outsiders ever get close to. The 4-metre-high stone statue known as *Ratu Gede* (or sometimes *Da Tonte*), standing inside its own seven-tiered *meru* pagoda, is one of the most closely guarded secrets on Bali. Trunyan has been inhabited for over 1,000 years, and *Ratu Gede* is believed to be even older. How it was transported here and from where, are just two of the many mysteries surrounding this ancient treasure.

The stone plays a central part in local mysticism but is rarely seen, except on the occasion when adolescent boys perform a ritual dance as part of their initiation to manhood. The temple – whose name could be translated as "navel of the universe" or "controller of the world" – is normally off-limits to visitors, but access is sometimes allowed if you are wearing a sarong. The closest you will be able to get to the stone god, however, will be next to the great stone boulder (draped with a black and white *poleng* cloth, symbolising balance) that protects the padlocked door of the *meru*.

The deep mysteries that surround this place are so closely guarded that local people refuse even to pronounce the name of the boulder.

The final resting place of the Hindus of the Wind

Despite Trunyan's isolation and the rough state of the road, the village regularly attracts tours. The only reason outsiders visit Trunyan at all is to see the famous cemetery, which is accessible only by boat and lies about half a kilometre around the shoreline from Trunyan. The people of Trunyan are Bali Aga and are known as "Hindus of the Wind": rather than bury their dead (as do Tenganan's Bali Aga, the "Hindus of the Earth") or cremate them, they simply lay the bodies out under bamboo cages under the sweet-smelling *taru menyan* tree, which disguises most of the smell of putrefaction.

Wayan Cipta guides visitors by rowing a boat to the cemetery. "It is the only thing that tourists want to see when they come here," Wayan says. "They don't realise that with our rich and unique cultural traditions, there are other things to see here."

LAVA FIELDS OF MOUNT BATUR ②

Walk through fields of fossilised fire

Unnamed road, best accessed from Jalan Raya Kintamani, Batur Selatan, Kintamani. Follow Google Maps directions to Bukit Payang

Mount Batur is probably best known as the destination for Bali's most popular trek: a pre-dawn climb to take in the sunrise. But to enjoy Batur's dramatic volcanic landscape in perfect solitude, simply head

for the immense lava fields below Kintamani. These virtually unvisited lava fields on the southern slopes of Mount Batur's peak are the result of an eruption that happened in 1968; they are a haunting, lunar-like landscape a world away from the forests, beaches and rice paddies for which Bali is so well known.

The fringes of the lava fields are easy to access by either car or motorbike, although the steep, winding descent from the Jalan Raya Kintamani ridge road may induce white knuckles. The lava fields are certainly not an ideal sunrise trekking spot, and even in full daylight you should take great care clambering over the razor-sharp boulders and deep crevasses – though it is very rewarding to be here and appreciate this harsh landscape.

The Balinese are fatalistic about the immense powers under their feet, and they accept that, like the god Siva (who is at once both the destroyer and the creator), the volcanoes are also the source of the rich agricultural land that covers the Kintamani highlands. When standing on the lava fields you gaze up to the summit of Batur and eastwards to the peak of Agung – the two mountains that are represented in the traditional *candi bentar* (split gateways) you see all over the island. It is said that Siva pulled the mythical Mount Meru apart to create Batur and Agung. Bear in mind that the great mass of black rock you're standing on is the result of what was, in geological terms, the mere popping of a pimple; it is impossible to comprehend the force behind the giant eruption that created Batur's 7.5km-long caldera lake some 30,000 years ago.

Every morning, trekkers begin a torchlight procession up the flank of Mount Batur. It's likely that most have little idea that they will be joining what is certainly Indonesia's biggest daily trekking event, with hundreds of other hikers intent on taking a selfie with the sunrise behind Mount Agung and, on a clear day, the peak of Rinjani on Lombok. The view is spectacular but the experience is far from spiritual, since the climb frequently comes to a standstill as the continuous queue of trekkers bottlenecks at particularly tight sections of the dangerously eroded trail.

The climb to the 1,717-metre-high peak is not too challenging, so some travellers choose to climb solo rather than pay any fees to the numerous companies operating out of Ubud. A local organisation tries to enforce the use of guides from the community. Their charges are usually reasonable, and with hundreds of people passing through their villages during the early hours of each morning, it seems only fair that the local community derives some income.

Indonesia is balanced precariously on a volcanic ridge that runs around the Ring of Fire, and has more volcanoes than any other country on earth, an estimated 127 of which are considered active. Batur is still periodically active and has erupted 27 times since its activity was first documented in 1804.

THE PLACENTA GRAVEYARD IN BAYUNG GEDE

3

A graveyard for the spiritual siblings of a village

Bayung Gede, Kintamani, Bangli

At the southern end of a village called Bayung Gede there is a small forest of trees unlike any other in the world. This forest is a sacred place for the people of the village; it is a graveyard for the placentas of every baby born in Bayung Gede.

Around Bali people consider the placenta to be the spiritual sibling of a newborn baby; they call it *ari ari*, which means "younger sibling" (because the placenta is "born" after the baby). Tradition around the rest of the island is to wash the placenta in flower-scented water then place it in a young coconut or a clay pot, along with some thorns to protect the *ari ari* from evil spirits. It is buried outside the family home; the placenta of a boy is buried on the right side of the entrance (if you're standing inside, looking out), while that of a girl is buried on the left, and for 42 days offerings are made and incense and candles burn over the pot.

Bayung Gede, however, follows a different tradition. Across the island, blood is considered unclean; the villagers of Bayung Gede maintain that if the placenta is buried near the home, a *mangku* (priest) wouldn't be able to enter when a ceremony needed to be performed. In order to get around this (and to keep the village "clean"), after washing the placenta in scented water and closing it inside a coconut, they hang it in one of the *bukak* trees in the forest on the southern edge of the village. The branches around the coconut are then cut in order to release a sap that will absorb the smell of decomposition.

Setra Ari Ari, the placenta cemetery, is a very quiet place. It's surrounded by a paved pathway and low wall, and the forest really does have a spiritual quality to it. Hanging from the trees throughout the forest are hundreds of coconuts clumped together on branches; there are coconuts around the base of the trees too, remaining where they fell after the natural fibres that held them tied up had disintegrated.

The village of Bayung Gede dates back almost 12 centuries. For much of this time it was surrounded by a sacred forest and remained fairly isolated. As a result, traditions such as the *ari ari* cemetery evolved here and nowhere else on the island.

The Balinese believe that *ari ari* is one of the *kanda empat*, the four siblings that protect the baby in the womb then stay with and guide a person throughout their life. *Ari ari* is the placenta, *yeh nom* is the amniotic fluid, *rah* is blood, and *lamas* is the *vernix caseosa*, the waxy, yellowish coating found on the skin of newborn babies. The *kanda empat* will protect the fifth sibling – the human – only if that sibling respects and looks after the *kanda empat* through ceremonies and acknowledgement.

ENDEK PRODUCTION IN TELAGA TAWANG ④

The woven fabric of a dying art form

Bali Arta Nadi, Jalan Semarpura-Karangasem, Telaga Tawang, near Sidemen, Karangasem
Daily 8am–5pm

The tradition of weaving runs deep in South East Asia, and the beautiful fabrics produced in the region are used not only for everything from everyday wear to ceremonies marking birth, death and marriages, but also to show social status. Around Indonesia, particular designs were, in the past, reserved for royalty, and the weaving was done only by the women of the palace. In Bali, *endek*, a type of *ikat* cloth, was traditionally made and worn only by members of the higher castes. *Ikat* is a cloth in which the pattern is created by tying a design onto the threads then fixing it through a process of reverse dying. Usually the design is created on the warp threads (those set on the loom running away from the weaver's body), but with *endek* fabric, the pattern is dyed onto the weft (the thread that runs from left to right).

Producing *endek* is no longer the domain of a particular caste and the fabric is now a favourite among many Balinese people – it's actually the fabric of choice for many uniforms. Said to have originated in Klungkung, Gianyar and Karangasem, *endek* is still produced by hand around the village of Sidemen, in the Karangasem regency. It's a complicated process that involves a number of people; two of these processes can be seen in the village of Telaga Tawang, close to Sidemen.

At a workshop called Arta Nadi you can watch the fabric being woven. But before you stop in there, walk past the workshop and continue a couple of hundred metres into the village where, at an unmarked pink house on the left-hand side of the road, the patterns are tied onto the weft threads. The tying here is done by young boys (outside of school hours) "because it's too difficult for girls to do," the villagers laugh. The weft thread is wound around a frame then marked with a pencil at one-inch intervals. This forms the grid on which the design is based.

The tying process is called *mebed* and is done these days with plastic raffia. In the past, palm leaves would have been used. Different coloured raffia indicates the dying stage at which the layers of plastic should be removed in order to produce the pattern.

Once the threads have been dyed (in a different village), they are returned to Telaga Tawang where the *endek* cloth is woven at Arta Nadi. The looms are set up with the base colour of the cloth running along the warp, and the women and girls (who learn the tradition during school holidays) then weave the dyed weft thread to make a sarong. Because they're weaving the pattern with the weft it's a more difficult process than if the pattern was already set up on the loom, and the weaver needs to adjust the thread each time the shuttle passes through in order to keep the pattern neat.

It will take around a day for the women to weave a 2-metre length of *endek* fabric (the length of a sarong), and these are sold in the Arta Nadi shop from Rp350,000 per sarong.

LONTAR PAGE WORKSHOP

⑤

"Leafing" through a traditional book

Dusun Tengah Sidemen, Karangasem
Private home: no charge but donations gratefully accepted

For centuries, important Balinese scripts have been written onto pages made from the leaves of lontar palms: from regular text to the rules of cockfighting (see page 188), to medicinal knowledge and the most sacred of religious text. Words and images have been very carefully drawn onto leaves that are strung together and concertinaed between two bamboo "covers". Thousands of these valuable manuscripts are kept in the Museum Gedong Kirtya in Singaraja, but what's not very well known is how the pages are actually made.

Working alone in his family compound in the hamlet of Tengah near Sidemen, I Gusti Ngurah Anom is one of the last people in Bali who makes these traditional pages. "It takes a lot of time and many processes," the old man says as he sits on his veranda surrounded by *tepesan*, the presses that clamp together the drying lontar pages. Ironically, not many lontar palm trees grow near Sidemen, so he buys the leaves, which have already been cut along the spines, from a supplier. While he can't always choose which leaves he works with, Ngurah, who has been making these lontar pages "since I got married", acknowledges that it's the older leaves that make better, stronger pages.

The process begins with the leaves soaking in cold water for four days. They're then boiled in water for one day and placed out in the yard to dry for another day – "I have to hope there is no wind, otherwise they scatter everywhere!" Once they've been sun-dried, the lontar leaves are then dealt with individually; each one is trimmed roughly to the size of the *tepesan* it will be dried in, and three holes – one in the middle and one near each end – are then "drilled" by hand into the leaf. Once the pages have been written on, the thread that binds the pages and allows them to concertina will be woven through these holes.

The leaves are clamped together in a big *tepesan*, handmade by Ngurah. They will remain there for two weeks before being moved to a smaller tepesan, where they will be pressed for a further three weeks. Before they're removed from this final press, the edges are planed to a smooth finish and painted red. Only once that paint has dried are the lontar released from the clamp.

At souvenir stores around Bali you're likely to see a Balinese calendar (see page 22) or scene from the *Ramayana* drawn onto a book of lontar leaves (see following page) ... and it's highly likely that those pages were handmade right here by I Gusti Ngurah Anom.

Seen from a distance, lontar palms *(Borassus flabellifer)* look like giant lollipops. They grow to around 30 metres in height and produce a crown of about 60 stiffly projecting fan-shaped leaves, which are used for thatching, making walls, weaving and making Cili, an effigy of the rice and fertility goddess Dewi Sri.

LONTAR BOOK WORKSHOP

⑥

A centuries-old tradition of producing traditional manuscripts

Griya Ulah, Sidemen, Karangasem
Ask in the village for the home of Ida Bagus Artamawa (there is no street address)
For classes in lontar art, contact Ida Bagus Artamawa: 0852 3726 1967

The village of Tenganan is widely known for the intricate lontar manuscripts that some villagers produce. But in east Bali, the village of Sidemen is also home to a handful of talented artists who continue the dwindling, intricate craft of making Bali's traditional books (see previous page).

"You have to be very careful when you are making them," says artist Ida Bagus Artamawa. He carefully draws onto the leaf "page" with a sharp blade in his right hand while steadying the blade with his left thumb. "If you make a mistake the whole lontar will be ruined."

The markings on lontar are made with a sharp blade then "inked" in when a burnt *kemiri* (candlenut) is rubbed onto the lontar and wiped off with a cloth. The oily candlenut ash is left behind in the grooves, colouring the markings that have been made black. "If I am inspired, I can create one manuscript in five days. If not, it will take a week," he says.

Ida Bagus Artamawa works on the veranda of his home, wearing a sarong as tradition requires. As well as producing lontar that has been commissioned by Balinese people, or that will be sold to tourists, he also teaches foreigners his craft. He makes it look easy, but the ridges in the pressed lontar leaves make it a very difficult art form for anyone used to drawing on smooth paper.

For generations, important information and stories have been kept on the leaves of lontar palms, to be read by priests, scholars, puppeteers and traditional healers. Written in curvy Bahasa Bali script, Sanskrit and Kawi (old Javanese), and usually without any illustrations, the lontar manuscripts would contain four lines of text on each side of the long, narrow page.

There are different classifications of lontar, divided according to the subjects dealt with in the manuscripts. *Weda*, for example, are the holy books, while *usada lontar* deal with healing and traditional medicine. *Prasi lontar* are illustrated lontar – most widely produced today due to tourist appeal – and the scenes drawn on these are derived from *wayang*, the shadow puppet plays.

The Gedong Kirtya library in Singaraja was founded by the Dutch government in 1928 and houses a large collection of lontar manuscripts that are collected, copied and preserved here. Jalan Veteran 23, Singaraja, Buleleng; open Monday–Thursday 7:30am–3:30pm; Friday 7am 12:30pm.

ARAK HOMEBREW

⑦

The oldest arak distillery in Sidemen

Jalan Semarapura-Karangasem, Telaga Tawang, Sidemen, Karangasem
0852 3830 8513
Open daily
Free, but donations gratefully accepted (or buy a bottle!)

A simple little moonshine shack behind a homestead at the end of a track in Telaga Tawang is the oldest *tempat mulang* (an *arak* distillery) in the Sidemen area. Despite its humble appearance, this family business has earned a reputation for brewing trustworthy, safe and surprisingly smooth *arak*. But you're unlikely to see drunkenness in Bali (at least among locals). This is due largely to Indonesia's policy of high taxation on alcohol. To counteract this, however, innovative Indonesians from all over

The islands produce several forms of local "moonshine". The most famous (and strongest) of these is *arak*. The name has been adopted as the common term for an entire spectrum of spirits, which are produced in many parts of Asia and the eastern Mediterranean from a vast variety of fruits, cereals, rice, coconut, palms or sugarcane.

"I know of at least 17 different types of local trees that you can make *arak* from," maintains Wayan Subrata, who is considered one of the finest producers of *arak* in the Sidemen area. "The simple coconut tree, however, is the best."

Wayan collects the sap from the young flowers of coconut trees early in the mornings. For two days he allows it to settle, with coconut husk for flavour, to let impurities sink to the bottom. Then the liquid is boiled for about eight hours in a *kekeb* (a timber-insulated cauldron). The distilled *arak* rises through a pipe in the top of the *kekeb* and is cooled as it passes through a barrel of water before dripping out of a bamboo pipe into a jerrycan in the form of clear spirit (around 30–50 per cent proof). The strongest "Class 1" *arak* is the first to emerge. "It is explosive," says Wayan, "but the second and third grades are weaker."

Although technically illegal, home-brewed *arak* is produced in semi-secret backcountry still shacks throughout much of Indonesia; it is tolerated in Bali for its use in ceremonies. There have been several scares in recent years when methanol-tainted *arak* has caused blindness and even death – in some cases through the consumption of legal, commercial *arak* sold in supermarkets. It is certainly unwise to buy *arak* from disreputable backstreet sources, but with reliable local information it is possible to sample this natural product in relative safety directly from the source. You might even be pleasantly surprised.

What's in a name?

Although frequently spelled "arrack", the traditional firewater hooch of Indonesia more often goes by the shorter spelling. Just to confuse matters, a totally different Middle Eastern drink (made from grapes and flavoured with anis) is also called *arak*. *Tuak* is the name given to the juice that comes from the flower stem of the aren tree (used in the production of palm sugar, see page 129). When first collected, *tuak* is not alcoholic and is reminiscent of sweet, tangy homemade lemonade, but it can also be fermented until it becomes alcoholic (although less potent than *arak*). Another drink that is often confused for both *arak* and *tuak* is *brem*, which is essentially rice wine. This is made from sticky rice that has been simmered for hours with yeast, then allowed to ferment for a few days. Both *arak* and *brem* are commonly used in temple offerings to placate the Bhuta Kala (the low spirits or demons).

KLUNGKUNG PUPUTAN MONUMENT

8

Monument to Bali's resistance heroes

Corner of Jalan Untung Surapati and Jalan Gajah Mada, Semarapura, Klungkung
Daily 8am–5pm
Rp50,000 per person includes entry to Museum Semarajaya, Kertha Gosa Klungkung, Puri Klungkung, Balai Budaya Klungkung

The name "Klungkung" echoes stolidly through the course of Balinese history as the kingdom before which all other kings bowed. The Klungkung Puputan Monument serves as a memorial not only to Klungkung's King Ida I Dewa Agung Jambe, but also to an estimated 200 unknown heroes of Balinese resistance (see page 28).

Unusually, this historic cenotaph is in the form of a 28-metre-tall *lingga-yoni*, a phallic symbol (see page 208). Perhaps the significance of this is that the *lingga-yoni*, also a symbol of Lord Siva, is a sign of rebirth and reincarnation – although it is believed that, as the ultimate honourable sacrifice, *puputan* is a means of achieving instant Nirvana. However, all of this is pure conjecture (as is the story of the *puputan* itself) as there is little information explaining the monument. Walk into the side door of the "yoni", and you will find a life-size statue of the king and some of his family and guards, surrounded by a circle of dioramas showing the last eras of the great Balinese kingdoms.

On 17 April 1908 King Ida I Dewa Agung Jambe, along with his entire family and his retinue of palace officials and guards, marched out to face insurmountable Dutch troops. The king was armed with his famous *keris* (see page 196), which, according to an ancient prophecy, should have made the Balinese force invincible. Not surprisingly, it wasn't enough, and the last independent kingdom in Bali fell to Dutch firepower. The king was cut down by Dutch bullets, whereupon, according to legend, six of his wives immediately performed *suttee* (the Hindu rite where a wife kills herself to follow her husband into the next life). Seeing this, the estimated 200 Balinese in the group also took their own lives. This form of ritual suicide – in preference to an ignoble surrender – is known in Bali as *puputan* and is something that recurred several times throughout the early years of Dutch intervention on the island.

In effect it is doubtful that anyone will ever know how many people really died in the *puputans*, since there were no Balinese survivors and it was such a shameful event to the Dutch that it was rarely mentioned in reports. Even the hardened troops (who, according to some eyewitnesses, looted the palaces and the royal corpses) were said to have been sickened by what they had seen. In 1906 a similar *puputan* took place in what is now Denpasar, and while some estimates say that as many as 3,600 Balinese may have died, the official Dutch report gave the body count as just 450. In a letter to his wife, Dutch artist Wijnand Otto Jan Nieuwenkamp (see page 180), who witnessed the "battle", called it a "disgusting massacre" and wrote that more than 1,800 Balinese people died, while the Dutch suffered only four fatalities.

SALT FIELDS OF KUSAMBA

⑨

Organic salt produced on a beach in east Bali

Jalan Raya Goa Lawan, Kusamba, Klunkung
Look for "natural salt maker" signs on the coastal road near Pura Goa Lawah

East of Amlapura (the capital of the Karangasem regency) there is a beach where, during the dry season, delicious salt is made using a process unchanged in decades. Across Bali, people consider the salt from this beach to be particularly tasty. It is even, according to a sign in a small salt store on the beach, "salt that has been evaluated as world's best taste".

Making this salt is a difficult and exceptionally labour-intensive process. It's a process you can witness if you follow the small handmade "natural salt maker" signs from along the road near Pura Goa Lawah. On this beach, a small community has been making sea salt for at least the past 70-odd years.

In the early morning, the salt makers collect and carry sea water in yoked containers – each weighing 30 kg – then splash it out onto a raked area of dark grey sea sand. This is repeated over and over. The sand, which is above the high tide line, is then left to bake in the sun for a few days. When sufficiently dry, the top layer of this now salty sand is collected and repeatedly rinsed with seawater in a series of coconut trunk vats. There are three vats, each producing brine that will become a different grade of salt. This brine, which is about 10 times saltier than seawater, is then transferred to shallow troughs that have been carved out from palm trunks. After two days, when the water evaporates, the white sea salt is left behind.

"When it rains, we rest," said one woman who has been making salt for 50 years. "Since I was very small I worked with my parents," she said. "The Japanese people showed us how." There is a rich history and tradition of salt making in Japan, where one of the oldest records of the industry dates back to the 8th century – although the tradition dates back much further than that.

The salt made on the beach at Kusamba is sold locally and bags of the mineral are usually available for sale at each salt maker's "distillery". A 1 kg bag of salt will set you back just Rp40,000 and makes a tasty souvenir. A sign in one of the salt maker's huts promises "Mysterious salt feels sweetness". And you'll notice that it does, indeed, have a slightly sweet flavour.

THE NATURAL DYERS' AND WEAVERS' COOPERATIVE OF SERAYA

10

Where heirloom fabrics are made

Banjar Dinas Kangin, Desa Seraya Timur, Karangasem
Daily 8am–6pm

In a little coastal hamlet along one of the most scenic roads in Bali there is a cooperative of dyers and weavers who are colouring cottons with natural dyes handmade from leaves, roots and flowers. They are also creating *rangrang*, a type of fabric that was on the verge of being forgotten forever. The Natural Dyers' and Weavers' Cooperative of Seraya is an open studio where visitors can watch the weaving and dying process, and take part in workshops to learn the skills themselves.

Seraya is a small village close to the far eastern tip of Bali. The land here is steep, dramatic even, and the view from the road that wraps around this peninsula (and from the weavers' cooperative) is sublime. From here the Indian Ocean stretches east to Lombok and south to Nusa Penida, an island with a rich tradition of weaving and dying – and it is a beautiful fabric native to Nusa Penida that the weavers in Seraya create.

Rangrang (which means "open" or "with holes") is a slit-tapestry woven cloth created on a backstrap loom called a *cagcag*. Unlike most fabrics, which are made with one continuous weft thread, *rangrang* is made from a bundle of wefts that are woven to create interlocking zigzags or diamond patterns, with small holes left as part of the design. According to Indonesian textile experts Threads of Life, "these filigree textiles with an open weave were used as breast wraps for ceremonial dances after it was determined women should not dance bare-chested."

This cooperative is one of only a few places on the island where natural dyes are made, and Pak Karya, who heads up the group, is considered among Indonesia's leading experts in natural dyes. "Just look at this colour!" he enthuses as he lifts a small cup of almost muddy brown liquid from a vat packed with indigo leaves. "It's not so blue yet because it needs to be oxygenated," he explains, giving the cup a swirl until the liquid turns a beautiful deep blue.

It's almost like a magic show, seeing how the dyes are prepared. Blue comes from the leaves of indigo trees; yellow from the skin of pomegranates; red is from the roots of morinda trees. Some colours will be boiled, others not, and at the end of the process, which could take four days, cottons in beautiful shades of reds, ochres, yellows, blues and browns emerge from the vats. "To make black it's a double process," explains Pak Karya. "You must dye the cotton blue and brown." Once the cottons have been dyed, the colour is set with vinegar derived from *tuak* (see page 162).

The fabrics are sold in the cooperative's small shop, and you can expect to pay from Rp400,000 for a small piece. Considering it's made and dyed by hand, it's a very reasonable price for an exquisite piece of art.

THE WALLACE LINE

11

A unique chance to drive alongside the Wallace Line

Jalan Kerangasem-Seraya, Karangasem

When naturalist Alfred Russel Wallace, a contemporary of Charles Darwin, explored the Indonesian archipelago, he observed that there seemed to be a line that divided the types of flora and fauna found on the islands. On the east of the line the habitat is similar to that of Australia, while to the west it is more Asian. This imaginary line became known as the Wallace Line; it slices through Indonesia between Borneo

and Sulawesi and between Bali and Lombok. There is one place on Bali, however, where you can quite literally see the Wallace Line.

The dramatic rollercoaster ride of the Karangasem-Seraya road snakes and winds, climbs and plummets alongside the brutal cliffs of Bali's far east. It is one of the most breathtaking roads on the island. Take a few minutes to stop, however, and you can appreciate what for 150 years many naturalists have considered one of the defining features on our planet. Less than 40 km offshore lie the hills of Lombok, and rushing in between – often like a churning river – are the ripping currents that have served as an insurmountable barrier to the passage of wildlife between Eastern and Western Indonesia.

Traditionally, Bali was the land of tigers, deer and monkeys, while on the opposite side none of these creatures existed (unless they were imported by humans). Not only were these awe-inspiring, vicious currents impassable, but the channel here is also so deep that it withstood the periodic ice ages when surrounding areas were linked by land bridges.

While Wallace visited Bali only briefly 160 years ago (see page 114), in subsequent years he travelled some 22,000 km throughout what would become Indonesia. His book, *The Malay Archipelago*, remains probably the most insightful travel book ever written about the region. The Welsh naturalist is also credited with coming up with the theory of evolution in tandem with Charles Darwin. While Darwin lies in state at Westminster Abbey, Wallace was buried in a small graveyard in Dorset. Bizarrely, his headstone is a fossilised tree that bears an unmistakable resemblance to a phallus.

Historians believe that the first ocean voyage in the history of mankind may have departed from somewhere around here (see page 140), but while staring at this swirling maelstrom, the heart lurches at the mere thought of launching a humble bamboo raft here. The tiny island of Gili Selang is connected at low tide to the main island with its own 40-metre-long land bridge, so technically it qualifies as Bali's most easterly point. Once around this curve on the Karangasem-Seraya road, you suddenly realise you're driving past sheltered coves. The beaches here seem almost to be piled with *jukung* outriggers (mostly fibreglass rather than wood). They lie upon the pebble beaches, like brightly painted driftwood, in such numbers that it's hard to imagine that there can be enough people in the tiny hamlets to man all these boats.

Half an hour later you're entering the coastline known as Amed and are likely to be lured into another stop by the shimmering reefs that (beyond the pull of that fearsome current) have become one of Bali's great diving centres. During his travels, Wallace discovered about 5,000 species that were unknown to science. How many more would he have found if he had snorkelled?

Central Bali

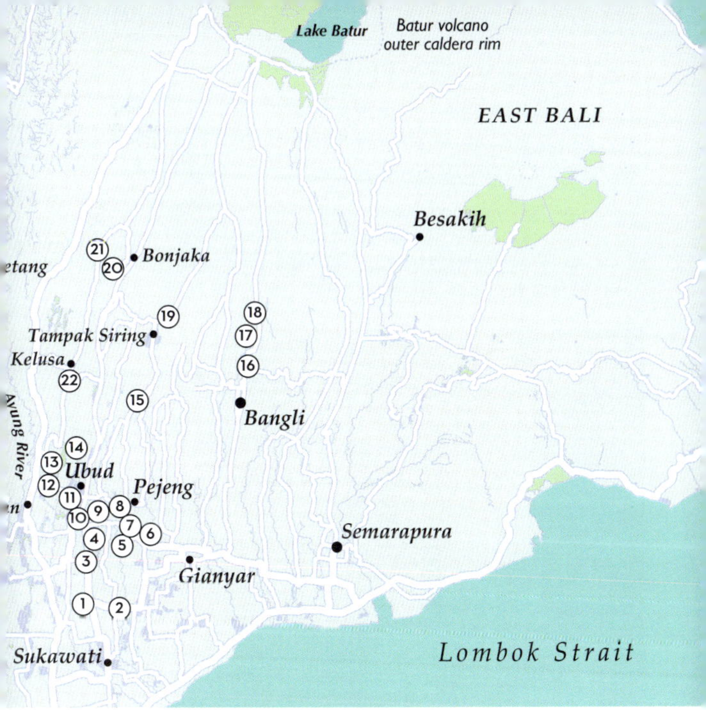
Lake Batur
Batur volcano
outer caldera rim
EAST BALI
Besakih
Bonjaka
Tampak Siring
Kelusa
Bangli
Ayung River
Ubud
Pejeng
Semarapura
Gianyar
Sukawati
Lombok Strait

FAT BABY STATUE

①

The geographic centre of Bali, a place to petition the spirits for a baby ... or something even more interesting?

At the crossroad between Sakah and Blahbatuh on Jalan Raya Sakah, Sukawati, Gianyar

Most locals will know this landmark as Patung Bayi Gemuk – the Fat Baby statue. They're also likely to tell you that this statue marks the geographic centre of the island. The area is often referred to as Blah Tanah (meaning "middle of the land"), but even a cursory glance at a map of Bali will show you that this is not true.

The 8-metre-tall statue sitting in the centre of the three-way junction is hard to miss. It was erected on a coral hummock transported here from the Bukit Peninsula. The "baby" might look very cherubic, cheerful, contented and (extremely) well fed, but there are countless tales of the statue being haunted. Local people claim that they sometimes hear it crying in the night (especially on the full moon), and passers-by are sometimes shocked by the impression that the statue has turned and is looking at them.

A security guard has the unenviable duty of guarding the spot at night, but according to the local priest, his job is primarily to protect the little copse of precious and sacred *pule* trees (see page 190) on the roundabout, rather than the statue itself. Jero Mangku Ketut Widiantara, who officiates as priest here (when he's not working on his other job at Garuda Indonesia's customer service desk at the airport), believes that the spirit in the statue is a benevolent one, since childless couples who have come here to petition the spirits for a baby have often had their wishes granted.

Although the statue is a relatively recent addition to Bali's heartland, mystery has surrounded it ever since it was commissioned by Gianyar regent Cokorda Darana in 1989. Other potential candidates for a memorial at the junction were a puppet (to commemorate a traditional craft that is still practised in this area) and freedom fighter Captain I Wayan Dipta (who is already memorialised at the nearby Bali United stadium), so local residents were surprised when the 8-metre-tall Fat Baby turned up on their doorstep.

The actual identity of the baby was only revealed a couple of years ago – and in true Balinese style, only after a suitably propitious day had been determined. In 2015 a descendent of the statue's donor told the *Tribun Bali* newspaper that the figure was installed as a dedication to Lord Shiva and that the Fat Baby's real name is Sang Hyang Brahma Lelare. He refuses, however, to shine any further light on the mystery. "It's very complicated and would take quite a while," he told the *Tribun* reporter.

It seems that the background to the Fat Baby is destined to remain a mystery for some time to come.

VIHARA AMURVA BHUMI BUDDHIST TEMPLE 2

An unexpectedly vibrant Chinese-style temple in the heart of old Bali

Jalan Darma Giri, Blahbatuh, Gianyar
0361 7435 550
Daily 8am–5pm
Free entry, donations appreciated if you take photographs

Chinese traders have been a part of life on Bali since long before the first European explorers set eyes on the Island of the Gods (in 1512). Chinese coins, still known as *kepeng* in Bali, have been in use for more than a thousand years; even today, replicas are still a central part of many Hindu offerings (see page 20).

The town of Blahbatuh (6 km south-east of Ubud) has been a business centre for a large community of Peranakan (as Chinese-descended Indonesians are traditionally known) for longer than anyone can remember. The Vihara Amurva Bhumi Buddhist temple in Blahbatuh is located on the edge of a shady jungle gorge on the Petanu River, under the old colonial-era bridge (now disused). You might not want to risk the rotten planks of the bridge, but it is worth a walk down the crumbling concrete steps to the riverbed for a brief spell of solitary meditation of your own.

The temple itself has traditional guardian lions, brightly painted dragons wrapped around the pillars, and a beautiful old tower for burning "god money". In contrast to the sacred banyan trees you find in so many Balinese temples, the back patio of Vihara Amurva Bhumi boasts a sacred Bodhi tree – similar to the one under which Buddha is said to have experienced his moment of enlightenment

The cemetery on the hill above the temple is an eerie place to explore and shows that the Chinese community here remains true to their heritage (although the names of recent generations are more reminiscent of Indonesia than of China). At the same time it is fascinating to see that unlike Buddhist temples in other parts of the island, many local Hindus come to pray at Vihara Amurva Bhumi. Specifically, it is believed that this is a powerful location in which to pray to ancestors, and the ideal spot to ask for protection at the start of a pilgrimage.

Anyone familiar with Bali knows that this is one of the most hospitable islands in the world and that Balinese Hinduism is one of the most tolerant religions. Balinese Hindus rarely subscribed to the persecution and discrimination that was common on other Indonesian islands.

ASTINA MASK GALLERY AND WORKSHOP

③

"When you wear a mask you are no longer yourself"

Jalan Raya Mas, Mas, Gianyar
081 338 448 444
balimaskmaking.com
Daily 8am–5pm

Behind an unassuming doorway that leads off a busy road in Mas village, not far from Ubud, there is a family compound where masks have been made for generations. According to Ida Bagus Anom Suryawan (renowned as one of the best mask makers in Bali), it is not something that one chooses to do; making topeng, as masks are called in Indonesian, is

one chooses to do; making *topeng*, as masks are called in Indonesian, is a calling.

Anom, whose uncle taught him to carve when he was nine, has masks in his gallery that range from fantastical Western theatre ones, through a range of traditional Balinese masks, to one that his grandfather carved – the most special one in Anom's collection (and it's not for sale).

While the gallery is a fascinating place to look around, or even to try your hand at carving if you've booked ahead, what is even more interesting is to hear about what goes into making the masks. "Every *topeng* that's used for ceremonial purposes has its own spirit, and there are so many processes that are involved in making these masks," says Anom, who observes the tradition of wearing *pakaian adat*, a ceremonial sarong, while working.

Before one can start to make a ceremonial *topeng*, a priest must first determine an auspicious day on which to source the wood. While masks that are created to become souvenirs are often made from hibiscus wood, ceremonial masks are made only from *pule* wood (*Alstonia scholaris*, see page 190) – a tree usually found near temples and graveyards. A branch cannot be cut down, however; it must fall naturally in order for the wood to be used for a mask. However, if the priest says the mask must come from a specific tree, then a piece of wood can be cut out from the trunk of the tree in such a way that the tree survives.

Once all of the ceremonies surrounding the wood have been performed, the priest will determine the auspicious day on which the craftsman should start carving the mask, as well as the date by which it must be finished. "It is not up to me to decide these things," shrugs Anom.

As well as being a master carver, Anom is a dancer and puppeteer, which, he says, is very useful to his art. "When you wear a mask you are no longer yourself; you become the mask," he explains. "Knowing and understanding this feeling is very important when making the *topeng*."

NEARBY

Setia Darma House of Masks ④

The Setia Darma House of Masks (Jalan Tegal Bingin, Mas; open 8am–4pm) could well be the most serene place in all of Ubud, and you're unlikely to see other visitors while you're here. Tucked into 1.5 hectares of beautifully landscaped gardens, six antique wooden buildings that have been collected from around Java house 1,300 masks and 5,700 puppets. The oldest puppet is around 1,000 years old, made from metal and formed in the shape of a leaf. Look out for the spectacular Reog Ponorogo mask, which has a real tiger's head mounted on it, along with dozens of peacock feathers. This mask weighs about 50 kg; it is worn by a man who shows his strength by holding the mask on with his teeth.

HORSE RELIEF AT YEH PULU ⑤

A 26-metre-long relief that may reveal links to India

Jalan Yeh Pulu, Blahbatuh, Bedulu, Gianyar
Daily 8am–5pm

It's easy for visitors who make the pretty 300-metre stroll along the Petanu River to imagine how it must have felt in 1925 when Wijnand Otto Jan Nieuwenkamp cleared the vegetation away to gaze upon the sculpted mural at Yeh Pulu. This relief – nearly 30 metres long by 3 metres high – remained hidden in a valley for more than 500 years before it was described to the world by the Dutch artist. Nieuwenkamp, the first Western artist to visit the island, was also probably the first person to import a bicycle to Bali; he was immortalised in 1906, astride his bike, on a temple wall in Kubutambahan.

What's fascinating about this relief is that it raises questions about the origin of horses in Bali. The theory long considered the most likely is that Bali's first horses were gifts to royalty from Chinese traders. If this were the case then the Bali pony (seen today pulling *dokar* carts in Kuta, Negara and Denpasar) would be descended from the tough ponies of the Mongolian steppes. The horse relief at Yeh Pulu, however, suggests a different origin.

Bali was trading with India long before the arrival of the Chinese. Indian pottery dating to 250 BC has been found here; the earliest known Chinese artefacts are newer by about 600 years. While allowances should be made for artistic license, the princely horse at Yeh Pulu bears a startling similarity to the regal warhorses of the Indian maharajas. The neck harness is of a type still used ubiquitously in India, but such harnesses are rarely, if ever, seen in Mongolia. Even artistic representations of Genghis Khan, who lived during the height of Chinese trade with Bali, never show his steed with such an ornate harness. Moreover, the Yeh Pulu horse's long ears are reminiscent of the Indian Marwari breed.

Equine experts often cite the fact that the tough hooves of Bali ponies do not need shoeing (although in practise most *dokar* carthorses are shod). While Mongol nomads habitually use steel shoes, the Marwari horses, which evolved on the stony plains of Rajasthan, are still renowned for the toughness of their hooves.

Legend has it that a giant called Kebo Iwa carved the Yeh Pulu relief with his fingernails, but in reality little is known about this archaeological treasure. The site typically raises more questions than answers for historians. Could it be true that the unknown artist of Yeh Pulu was a homesick exiled Indian?

CANDI TEBING TEGALLINGAH

⑥

Mysterious secluded ruins in central Bali

Tegallingah Village, Bedulu, Blahbatu, Gianyar

The ancient temple of Candi Tebing Tegallingah is hard to find. Even once you get to Tegallingah village's parking area, you need to look for a small pathway that leads directly west beside an old compound. You cross a little bridge between paddies and a forested ravine then begin a steep descent down 164 crumbling stone steps into a canyon. The network of channels, sluices and pools that fringe the paddies here are a fascinating insight into the Subak system (see page 73), the Balinese science of irrigation, which has been perfected over more than 1,000 years.

By the time you're within sight of the shadowy floor of the canyon, you will be aware of the channelling power of millions of years of pitiless tropical rainy seasons. You have to step cautiously over slippery boulders; the last section of steps was carried away years ago by floods, making access to the valley floor very risky indeed (and nearly impossible after rainfall).

Nevertheless, as you reach the lower levels and cross the rim of a slippery waterfall, you'll find yourself in sight of one of the oldest and most dramatic temples on the island. The site supposedly dates back to the 12th century; it is hard to imagine the labour that must have gone into carving the nine meditation niches and three temples into the canyon bedrock. The builders and rulers who commanded them are long forgotten, and most of the story behind Candi Tebing Tegallingah is likely to remain a mystery.

An excavated platform provides what seems to be an area for worshippers below a ledge where two sets of sacred *linggu* (phallic symbols) are believed to represent the Hindu trinity of Brahma (god of creation and fire), Wisnu (god of prosperity) and Siva (at once the creator and the destroyer).

While a timber footbridge crosses the Pakerisan River to the meditation niches in the opposite ledge, it is worth careful consideration as to whether the climb down the slippery moss-laden rocks is worth the risk. It would certainly be advisable for solo explorers to resist the temptation, since a slip could mean several painful days before another visitor (or worshipper) passes this way.

The more famous ancient temple complex at Gunung Kawi was only discovered in 1920, and Candi Tebing Tegallingah remained hidden from the outside world for almost 1,000 years. Even today, surrounded only by the sound of cascading water and jungle life, it is easy to imagine what it might have been like for the explorers who first set eyes on the shrouded mysteries of the bigger "undiscovered" temples of Borobudur and Angkor Wat.

LEMPAD CARVING AT BEDULU CONFERENCE CENTRE ⑦

The forgotten work of art by Bali's finest artist

Opposite Pura Samuan Tiga, Jalan Pura Samuan Tiga, Bedulu, Blahbatuh, Gianyar

I Gusti Nyoman Lempad was a man of many spectacular talents (not least among them was that he foretold the date of his death: 25 April 1978), and he is often cited as the most talented Balinese artist of all time. His work forms the pride of art collections at Agung Rai and Neka art museums in Ubud, as well as in virtually every celebrated fine art collection on the island – and yet few people are aware that one of his most spectacular works can be viewed for free, and almost certainly in solitude, at the Bedulu Conference Centre, an abandoned building across the road from a rarely visited temple in Bedulu village, less than 3 km from Ubud.

Not only was Lempad a great painter, he was also known as an *undagi* master, meaning that he was celebrated for his skill and knowledge of traditional architecture, carving, mask making, cremation artistry and sculpting. Lempad was already 106 years old when, in 1968, he began work with his nephew I Gusti Nyoman Sudara on the intricate 15-metre-long bas-relief on the terracotta outer wall of the Bedulu Conference Centre. The mural features scenes from a 14th century Javanese Buddhist poem called *Kakawin Sutasoma*, the poem that was the source of the motto of modern Indonesia, "Unity in Diversity". It was a fitting subject for this Suharto-era cultural centre, which was intended to be used for meetings by visiting politicians; "Unity in Diversity" was a favoured rallying cry of President Suharto.

Although the centre has been abandoned, visitors who take the time to hunt the site down will have the privilege of viewing an unexpected legacy from the man that Australian film-maker John Darling, who co-directed the documentary *Lempad of Bali*, called "the epitome of the complete Balinese artist and man."

As with so many Indonesians of his generation, it is not clearly established exactly when Lempad was born, but the great artist picked his day of death with almost mathematical precision. Three temples that had played a big part in his life were celebrating their *odalan* (birthday) ceremonies simultaneously: one was the all-powerful Besakih state temple, another the Pura Dalem (death temple) of his home village, and the third was Pura Samuan Tiga (over the road from the abandoned centre), where he had carved the great gate in 1955. The dilapidated *kulkul* tower (like a Balinese bell-tower) on the hill just above the cultural centre was another of his creations, and was probably ringing out his death knell that day.

PURA KEBO EDAN

8

An ancient fertility statue with "more than the usual quota of penises"

Jalan Raya Tampaksiring, Bedulu, Blahbatuh, Ubud, Gianyar
0361 942 354
Daily 8am–5pm
There's a visitor's book to sign and donations should be made

Pura Kebo Edan might seem like "just another Hindu temple" at first glance, but inside there is a mysterious statue that might be a god (some say Siva, others say Bima); it might be a demon; and it might bring happiness to couples who've been struggling to conceive.

Made Indah owns a little antique stall in the alleyway beside Pura Kebo Edan temple, and she is very happy to guide visitors around, since business here is invariably slow. Inside the temple's main compound, the statue in question is wrapped with a black and white *saput poleng* sarong around its bottom half.

"It's because he's shy," Made Indah says with a smile, "but he won't mind if I show you." A whole system of unusual fertility beliefs has been established around the Kebo Edan temple based on the bunch of stone penises that Made has just revealed. "See? He has four penises," she says, pointing to what seems to be just a swollen mass of stone around the statue's groin.

Made claims that the statue is of the god Siva, but it also might be Bima (the legendary hero of Balinese mythology). Other sources say it is a demon known as the Pejeng Giant, and that he has six penises not four. It is indeed hard to count since there seems to be a fair bit of deformity – not surprising, as the statue is believed to be about 700 years old.

One legend has it that Bima was unable to consummate his relationship with the woman he loved because his penis was too big. When she left him for a suitor of more manageable proportions, Bima killed his rival in a fit of jealousy. The unfortunate lover can be seen under the feet of the stomping giant.

Although Made believes that the statue is of Siva, she seems to think the four penises would be more useful on Bima. "Siva is married to Parwati," she explains, "and he is very faithful because she can be terrible if angry. But Bima is fair game because he has a reputation for liking the ladies."

Pura Kebo Edan means "Crazy Buffalo Temple", and either side of the main statue you find the two sculpted buffalo that gave the temple its name. Every year in the days before Galungan (Bali's bi-annual celebration), many people come here to collect water, which they will then use to bless their livestock.

Want to become more intelligent?

On the other side of the temple courtyard there is an ancient statue of the elephant-headed god Ganesha (Siva's son). Legend has it that if you stroke his forehead you will become more intelligent.

The statue that could impregnate barren women

Another prevalent local myth is that the temple's multi-faceted main statue has the ability to impregnate barren women. Made Indah claims that in recent years even Japanese couples have come here to make offerings in the hope that they will be granted a baby. Apparently, it's not necessary to stroke anything.

PELIATAN COCKFIGHTING ARENA ⑨

Skip the blood and gore but check out a Balinese gladiator arena

Jalan Sukma Kesuma 76–80, Peliatan, Ubud, Ginayar
Daily – cockfights often take place Friday–Sunday

Unlike most rural cockfighting areas, which are simply a cleared dust patch among the houses or a semi-secret shelter out in the paddies, the Peliatan Cockfighting Arena is a purpose-built open-sided barn, albeit with a metal fence to protect onlookers from the razor-sharp steel spurs that serve as twin swords for the feathered gladiators.

"It's hard to know when there will be cockfighting," says Ibu Nyoman, who runs a tiny carving workshop across the road from the arena. "There's no set fixtures, but word goes around pretty quickly, and sometimes there can be a couple of hundred men here."

Ibu Nyoman claims that amongst the crowd there will only ever be a few women, and they will only be there as hawkers and cooks. Casting a glance sideways at her husband, she whispers that while many men like to gamble, women only use their money for food.

It is indeed true that gambling is often an important part of macho identity for many Balinese males. Leaving aside the obvious Anglo-Saxon parallels, it is true that a man who pits his favourite rooster in the ring will often feel that his manhood is on the line. The excitement surrounding a bout is intense, but for the onlookers it is focused on the win-or-lose aspect of gambling rather than the brutal battle for life and death on the packed earth of the arena floor. Complex hand signals are used to place bets at moments when voices could never rise above the din.

While cockfighting is technically illegal in Indonesia (since 1981), the law is often not enforced in Bali; authorities realise the near impossibility of prohibiting an ancient ritual that is a central part of many religious ceremonies. In 1928 a cockfighting fund-raiser lasting for 12 days was held at Besakih Temple, the most important temple on the island.

As long as 1,000 years ago, cockfighting was already so well organised as to be taxable, and it was a form of ritual bloodletting that served for purification long before that. Each year in the Bali Aga village of Tenganan, young men fight with sharp pandan leaves in a similar ritual that involves the letting of human blood. These rituals draw hundreds of tourists, yet very few ever choose to witness the barbarity of cockfighting. What is unusual about custom-built cockfighting arenas such as this one at Peliatan is that it stands as a tacit admission that Bali's favourite blood sport is as much a social institution as a religious one.

The roosters are trained gladiators, fed chilli to make them "angry", spending much of their time in woven baskets on the roadside so that they become accustomed to noise and human activity. Drive a few miles on a cool afternoon and you'll see cockfighting baskets lining every road, and you'll realise that this blood sport is even more popular here than soccer.

PULE TREE OUTSIDE MONKEY FOREST 10

Cure your sore throat and ease your tired muscles

Jalan Monkey Forest, Ubud, Gianyar
Daily – the Monkey Forest itself opens 8:30am–6pm

What with marauding bands of thieving monkeys, few (if any) of the thousands of visitors who arrive at Ubud's famous Monkey Forest ever spare a glance for the majestic tree that looms over the car park. It is a *pule* tree (*Alstonia scholaris*), and this species is one of the most mysterious of Bali's big trees.

"*Pule* are among the most useful trees on the island," says Mangku Ketut Widiantara, a Hindu priest who lives near Ubud. "Every part of the tree can be used for medicine, and the soft, light wood is traditionally used for making masks" (see page 178).

This is perhaps fitting since the milkwood pine – sometimes called white cheesewood – is believed to contain the spirit of Durga, goddess of death. Another name for *Alstonia scholaris* is "devil tree"; in Sri Lanka, its wood is often used for making coffins.

Occasionally a *pule* tree becomes "pregnant" and the knobbly timber growth that appears on the trunk is particularly sought after for making masks, especially those portraying the demon-witch Rangda. Whenever *pule* trees are felled, offerings must first be made to placate the spirits in the tree. Even if you only want to remove enough to make a mask (which can be done without killing the tree), a complex ceremony must first be completed and a specially qualified priest will have to discern the best date for the "operation". To prepare the wood for carving into the most important ceremonial masks, it must be boiled in a mixture of tobacco and other plants for 42 days (with men working round-the-clock in shifts to stoke the fire).

Local healers claim that juice from *pule* leaves, when mixed into a drink with roasted coconut and palm sugar, is a cure for sore throats, and that the pounded bark can be dampened with water to ease tired muscles. Modern science has shown that the leaves do indeed have antibiotic properties, and that the bark contains bitter alkaloids to deter insects.

A tree that is impossible to plant

Unfortunately, despite traditional medicinal properties, the Balinese believe that *pule* trees are very hard (if not impossible) to transplant. "Nobody knows how the trees got to the spots where they grow," priest Ketut Widiantara explains, "because the strange thing about *pule* trees is that it's impossible to plant them. They always seem to plant themselves, and for some reason they prefer locations like temples, cemeteries and shrines."

FLUTE-PLAYING PIGEONS OF UBUD

11

Musical pigeons serenade Ubud town centre just after sunrise

I Made Marta family compound, Jalan Goutama Selatan, Ubud, Gianyar
Private home: viewing usually possible in the sky above central Ubud around 7am–9am and 5pm–6pm

Even many Ubud locals are unaware of the source of the strange whistling that seems to emanate from the sky on clear highland mornings. But gaze long and hard into what seems to be an impenetrable blue and you might see the sound's source: a small flock of pigeons banking with the shifting wind.

"I used to have about 100 homing pigeons," says the softly spoken I Made Marta as he stands beside a rack of bamboo cages enjoying his first cigarette of the morning. "But now I only have 30."

Made's family moved here from his village in Karangasem 25 years ago when he was just a child, but they introduced a hobby so rarely seen in Ubud these days that most young locals are completely unaware of it. Made cranes his neck up towards the sky, watching 14 of his pigeons descending in a spiral to the swooping tune of the little bamboo flutes (known as *sawangan*) that the birds wear around their necks. There is a look of rapture on his face.

"*Sawangan* can be made of bamboo, wood or steel, but bells are common too," Made explains. "The best is carved out of hollow goat bone and it makes a nice deep sound."

Every morning and evening, when the weather is clear, Made releases his birds. While they tend to fly for up to two hours, unexpected winds can often carry them as far as Denpasar, and it's been known for them to take a couple of days to return home. Made has Javanese pigeons (recognisable by their stocky necks) and Balinese pigeons (which have little feather tufts at the back of their heads). He claims that his best bird is worth around Rp200,000, and that his oldest is eight years old. A good pigeon can be a solid investment, since among Bali's homing pigeon aficionados this is a form of light-hearted gambling.

"There are a couple of other owners in this area," Made explains. "If, for example, my birds manage to entice a few away from another flock to come home here, then those birds belong to me. If, on the other hand, any of my birds leave and go to his coops, he would keep them, or if I wanted them back, I would have to go and pay him."

The origin of the flute-playing pigeons

It is believed that the tradition of flute-playing pigeons dates back to the 17th century when Taiwanese soldiers carved whistles for messenger pigeons. It is not known when the tradition became popular in Bali, but it remains one of the secrets of an Ubud highland morning, and continues to charm any visitors who take the time to allow their senses to veer heavenwards.

WALTER SPIES' HOUSE

⑫

Legendary artist and libertine Walter Spies, a founder of Ubud's artistic legacy

Hotel Tjampuhan Spa, Jalan Raya Tjampuhan, Ubud, Gianyar
0361 975 368
tjampuhan-bali.com
The house accommodates four people and costs about US$200 per night

"Just inside the doorway of Walter's living room was a space flooded with light reflected down from the open eaves," wrote Nigel Barley in his 2009 novel *Island of Demons*. "It was here that his new paintings were publicly auctioned."

Absolutely enthralled by all things Balinese, German artist Walter Spies is remembered as the earliest – and greatest – foreign influence on Ubud's art scene. During the decade that Spies lived here from 1930, his little house, overlooking Campuhan Ridge (in old Dutch spelling, *Tjampuhan*), entertained Charlie Chaplin, Miguel Covarrubias, Colin McPhee, Vicki Baum and millionaire socialite Barbara Hutton (for whom the pool – now a lotus pond – was apparently constructed).

The two-bedroom house stands in the grounds of what is now Hotel Tjampuhan Spa, and is available for rent; if it's unoccupied, the staff might let you take a quick look around.

Driven by demons of his own, Spies suffered from mood swings and intermittent depression. Legend has it that his Balinese neighbours attributed this to the fact that his house had been built with its roof higher than the temple on the other side of the ridge. If you stand in the open living room where Spies' semi-tame monkeys (and friends) once frolicked, this does indeed seem to be true. But Spies apparently refuted this, claiming that he had it surveyed and that it was merely an optical illusion.

Ill fate certainly seems to have had a hand in Spies' ultimate demise. Arrested as a possible German spy during World War II, he was being transferred from a prison camp in Sumatra when his ship was hit by a Japanese bomb (the Japanese, however, were presumably unaware that they were bombing German allies). The crew had orders not to evacuate their prisoners and Walter Spies was among the majority who died.

An escape from Ubud

When life in Ubud became a little too social, Walter Spies would escape to his quiet getaway in Iseh, near the pretty village of Sideman, from where he had an exceptional view of majestic Mount Agung. Austrian novelist Vicki Baum drafted part of *Love and Death in Bali* in this house; musician Colin McPhee and director Roman Polanski were also visitors here; and both Mick Jagger and David Bowie have subsequently stayed in what is now called Villa Iseh (www.villaiseh.com).

KI PIJETAN KERIS

13

The legends of "The Venerable Pinched One"

Neka Art Museum, Jalan Raya Campuhan, Ubud, Gianyar
0361 975 074
museumneka.com
Monday–Saturday 9am–5pm; Sunday noon–5pm
Entry: Rp75,000 per adult; children under 13 free

Among the 300 ceremonial swords and daggers in Neka Art Museum's Keris room there is one mysterious black-bladed weapon known cryptically as the Ki Pijetan, the "Venerable Pinched One".

Far from being a confession that it was acquired by unscrupulous means, it's believed that when it was forged in the 13th century, legendary blacksmith Mpu Geni Sandang Jiwa repeatedly pinched the red-hot blade with his bare fingers to create the rare markings known as *Pulo Tirta* (*Islands in Holy Water*).

In the world of symbolism and legend that surrounds the art of *keris*-making there is very little in the construction of one of these heirloom works of warrior art that could be considered purely ornamental. Everything in this sword has its reason – from the blade design known as "starling bird mattress essence" to the handle, said to be modelled on a cylindrical betel nut container and wrapped in a cord of human hair.

The "Venerable Pinched One" is unusual furthermore in that the hilt is an extension of the blade itself, and the *Pulo Tirta* markings – which are indeed reminiscent of a chain of coral atolls – were said to bring prosperity, social ease and family peace to the owner. The ivory crosspiece on the sheath was of a kind reserved for royalty; this *keris* originally resided at Gianyar's Puri Agung Mandangan Palace until it was finally sold by the family there in 1995.

Even today it is believed that the forgers of ceremonial *keris* must have sufficient priestly power to breathe actual life into these unique daggers. But locals will tell you that the fire-handling knowledge of master smiths like Mpu Geni Sandang Jiwa (whose name means "Fire Borne in the Soul") are lost to modern generations.

To the uninitiated, a Balinese (or Javanese) *keris* is usually recognised by the waving blade that symbolises a *naga* (dragon) in motion. Similarly, a straight blade – like that of the "Venerable Pinched One" – represents a dragon at rest; a dormant power that's ready to spring into action.

While historically many *keris* were created as weapons, their use in the recent past has more often been spiritual, although that does not mean they no longer draw blood. In the famous Barong dance, the witch-queen Rangda curses male dancers, puts them into a trance and orders them to commit suicide. The entranced dancers will often stab themselves with their own *keris* ... but it all ends well when Barong defeats Rangda, restores peace and magically heals wounds.

WIDYA BATIK WORKSHOP

⑭

Bright batiks created with natural dyes

Widya Batik, Jalan Sri Wedari no. 61, Tegallang, Ubud, Gianyar
0361 900 0633 or 081 7976 4154
widyabatik.baliklik.com
Daily 10am–5pm
Entry is free; a half-day class (10am–3pm) costs Rp450,000 and you get to keep the batik
Free transport to classes is offered from the Ubud area

Batik was born in the Javanese palaces of Solo and Yogyakarta, and was only adopted relatively recently in Bali. On this island of crisp sunshine and tropical blooms it quickly blossomed into a vibrant art form, very different to the subdued browns and dark blues of Java's textiles. Like the art form itself, Widya Harsana came to Bali from Solo.

"Here in Bali people like bright colours and big designs with a really tropical feel," he says. "The sombre autumnal colours of Central Java don't really do well on an island where it seems always to be bright summer."

While chemical dyes are almost universal even in Java's most traditional batik houses, Harsana is almost unique in preferring to use 100 per cent natural dyes. With its reputation as a holistic wellness Mecca, Ubud has nurtured a demand for natural-dye batiks; Harsana offers classes not just in batik art, but also in the use of natural dyes.

He produces a palette of 19 basic colours using a whole range of natural ingredients: rambutan skin or dragonfruit to produce red ink; indigo for blue; juice of teak leaf to create pink; fig leaves for black (actually very dark brown); green from pandanus leaves. The entire process is almost magical, since some of the colours react to sunlight and change. Harsana starts painting a design with what seems to be clear water but within less than a minute the turmeric in the dye has turned a vibrant orange in the afternoon sunshine.

"We have to buy our dyes from Java," Harsana admits, "because we don't have many of the ingredients here and there are few people who know how to produce the colours."

With the versatility and innovation that's typical of their island, Balinese batik artists invented not only new methods, but also new tools that were ideally adapted to their own style of batik, in which big colourful forms replaced the intricate repetitions of Javanese batik. To colour the sweeps of spreading petals and curling leaves, the Balinese use a brush made from the flattened tip of a bamboo sliver, which is smashed with a hammer and soaked in water until the fibres separate. Harsana demonstrates how this brush, known here as a *kuas bambu*, is capable of producing an attractive graduated colour or, when used end on, is equally well suited to producing a fine line.

Harsana tends to create a single large handmade batik per month. Often they are specific commissions from international collectors and fetch a price of around US$200 each. He supplements this income with drop-in classes from occasional foreign visitors who come to spend a few hours (sometimes even an entire month) learning batik skills from a traditional master.

OGOH-OGOH "MONSTER HIGHWAY" (15)

Warrior-monsters fit for the cover of a Marvel comic

Jalan Raya Tampaksiring, Tampaksiring, Gianyar
Best visited in the month before and after Nyepi

Nyepi is Bali's famous "Day of Silence" (see page 24), on which all transport (including air travel) ceases and everyone on the island has to stay indoors without making noise, light or smoke for 24 hours. The weeks building up to the great Ngrupuk processions of Nyepi eve are a time when the island's youths let their imaginations run wild. The great Ogoh-Ogoh effigies that appear all over the island in these weeks are typically the leeringly ravenous demons from the Hindu epics.

Along Jalan Raya Tampaksiring and in neighbouring villages, however, the local kids seem to have a very *Marvel*-esque way of viewing their demons. For any fan of old-time superhero comic books, a drive up this road is like cruising along a catwalk of iron-muscled warriors and snarling monsters. They have been built mostly by local teenagers who raised funds from the community for the bamboo framework, papier-mâché, paint, fabric and other materials.

In recent years, many Ogoh-Ogoh have been made from foam and polystyrene – unfortunate since the demon parade traditionally terminates in the Ogoh-Ogoh being burnt as a form of purification (somewhat ironic when the toxic black smoke starts to swirl) – but the government is now trying to ensure that only natural materials are used.

While Nyepi is an ancient ceremony, the Ogoh-Ogoh tradition started around the early 1970s, and by the mid-1980s the government was carefully monitoring them for disrespectful resemblance to the nation's leaders. This is very much a contemporary art form that remains subject to the whims (and competitive spirit) of teams of youths in neighbouring villages. Some spectacular Ogoh-Ogoh are on permanent display at Mengwi's Ogoh-Ogoh Museum (see page 226), but the rampaging beasts that appear along Tampaksiring's "monster highway" could well be Bali's finest example of this unique art form.

Ogoh-Ogoh are best seen in the month leading up to Nyepi when building is underway. But even after Nyepi, some of the best examples are left standing as exhibits by builders who couldn't bear to destroy their art. A new crop of Ogoh-Ogoh are potentially on view along the road through Tampaksiring every year for around two or three months, making this one of the world's best unofficial street art exhibitions. Some of the fi-nest creations would be worthy of display in any museum of modern art.

GIANT TREE AT PURA KEHEN 16

Bali's biggest tree ... probably

Pura Kehen, Jalan Sriwijaya, Cempaga, Bangli
Daily 8am–5pm

The Balinese find strong symbolism in great trees; trees that stand with their roots embedded in the underworld, and mighty trunks that reach through the domain of humans up towards the heights that are the home of the gods. Around the island there are trees that for generations have been considered sacred, and the biggest of them all could well be the spectacular fig tree *(Ficus benjamina)* at Pura Kehen in Bangli.

The tree's branches create a vast canopy that stretches out across the sacred grounds; there is a ceremonial "treehouse" *bale* high in its branches. This fig tree stands in the outer sanctum of the temple, called the *jaba*, and reaches across 55 metres; its circumference is more than 150 metres.

The people of Bangli believe that if one of the tree's branches breaks, someone in the community will soon die. The position of the broken branch will foretell who will pass away: if a branch breaks on the north-eastern side of the tree, for example, a king will die; if the branch is on the north-west, the person will be a Brahmin (high class); branches that break on the south-east or south-west indicate that a common person from the village will die.

The great fig at Kehen is often estimated to be somewhere between 400 and 700 years old. So was the tree planted after the temple was established or was the positioning of the temple influenced by the presence of a remarkable shade tree? We can't be sure, but if the latter seems more logical then the spectacular Kehen fig would have already been an adult tree when the temple was built around 800 years ago.

There are several candidates for the largest fig trees on the island: the sacred tree in the centre of Bengkala (see page 134) has a diameter of about 40 metres; at Bunut Bolong (see page 58) a fig tree covers the entire road, leaving only a tunnel for traffic under its 48-metre canopy.

Although *Ficus benjamina* (known in Indonesia as *beringin*) is the most common sacred tree, the mighty *Alstonia scholaris*, known as *pule* (see page 190), and *Ceiba pentandra (kapok)* also often form the spiritual and physical high points of Balinese temples. Often they're wrapped in the black and white chequered cloth called *saput poleng*, which symbolises harmony between the different realms of the world in much the same way that the tree represents a monument to the laws of balance that govern the universe.

BAMBOO ROOFS OF PENGLIPURAN VILLAGE

17

An enchanting village of jigsaw bamboo roofs

Penglipuran, Bangli

'We use bamboo for roofing in our village because we have so much bamboo in our area," Ibu Ketut Sudiasih shrugs. All over Indonesia you find entire villages constructed of bamboo, but the iconic tiled bamboo roofs of Penglipuran village are unlike any found elsewhere in the world.

At first glance, the layered bamboo strips of the older roofs look like shaggy tousled hairstyles. A closer look at the tiling system shows how the individual bamboo tiles are slit so that they can be slotted onto horizontal struts (without the need for nails or pegs), forming a layer that is impenetrable by the rain. "Even in the neighbouring villages you never find this style of roof," Ibu Ketut continues. "It's a system that works well, though, and our roofs can last for 25 years."

The main cobbled thoroughfare that runs north to south up the centre of Penglipuran might seem regimental when you first arrive, but this is one of Bali's most hospitable villages. It has become an established part of the tourist trail in this fairly rural part of Bali, and when you park outside the village you are likely to be approached to pay the (minimal) entrance fee. Few visitors seem to notice the strange bamboo roofs, and even anthropologists who have come to study the village's unique culture over recent years seem not to have noticed the architecture.

Nevertheless, most of the ornate ceremonial gateways leading off the main thoroughfare into the family compounds are roofed using this traditional system, and if you visit the family compounds (you're sure to be invited into one or two homes) you might see that the older traditional *dapur* kitchens are also constructed the same way.

This staunchly religious community boasts more than a dozen village temples (not counting individual family ones). Even by Balinese Hindu standards this is an impressive amount for a village with less than 1,000 inhabitants.

Locals claim that their village is named from a phrase that described the emotions of the Bangli king in the days when this cool highland village (located about 675 metres above sea level) was a royal retreat. "They say that the king was always happy to arrive," Ibu Ketut explains, "but sad when he had to leave."

Even today Penglipuran frequently affects visitors in the same way.

BAMBOO FOREST NEAR PENGLIPURAN

18

A natural cathedral of shady walkways that is protected by ancient taboos

Jalan Penglipuran, Kubu, Bangli

The sacred bamboo forest near Penglipuran village (see page 204) is in many ways a living cathedral: great curving arches straddle the pathway and light flickers through filmy leaves like sunrays through stained glass.

Although bamboo can be found growing all over Bali, the people of Penglipuran village claim that their ancestors originally planted this forest as a protection from landslides on these highland slopes. The sacred bamboo forest is carefully harvested to supply a sustainable crop as well as a protective barrier around the village. As a symbol of local heritage, it is protected from harm by strict taboos.

Life without bamboo would be difficult for rural Balinese people. It is used to build boats and rafts, and to produce farming implements, irrigation pipes, tools, woven *bedeg* mats, baskets, furniture, cooking pots, offerings and a score of different musical instruments (like the bamboo *tingklik* xylophone). Bamboo can be cut to fit together – like God's Meccano set – in perfectly organic ways, so that complex roof structures and even entire buildings can be assembled without the use of a single nail. It's so strong, resilient and easily replaced that cities like Hong Kong have returned to using bamboo scaffolding in the construction of high-rise buildings.

The symbolism of bamboo is intricate; when a body is buried (awaiting cremation) a bamboo pillow is used to allow the spirit to escape, and bamboo towers up to 20 metres high carry the deceased to the last rite.

What do waves and bamboo have in common?

Penglipuran's bamboo is harvested when it is about two years old. Local workers relate to three particular varieties: *petung* (strong bamboo used for building), *jajang* (lighter, used for roofing), and *tali* (the finest, used for weaving). There is a careful selection process to ensure sustainability, and according to local tradition, cutting should only be done after the rains and during the full moon. Scientific research conducted in India (by S. Dhawan and S.C. Mishra in 2005) confirmed that this is the best time, since the gravitational pull of the moon has an effect on the sap and starch content in plants in much the same way that it governs the tides. The effect is infinitesimal, but it was enough for the bamboo harvesters of Penglipuran to have noticed it.

A new species of bamboo discovered in 2004

There are more than 1,400 different species of bamboo in the world. In 2004 a new giant species – *Gigantochloa aya* – was discovered in Penglipuran. The botanical world was stunned to realise that a new species (growing up to 15 metres tall) had been hidden all this time in a forest in Bali.

LINGGA-YONI STATUE AT PURA TIRTA EMPUL

⑲

Phallic statues for the gods

Pura Tirta Empul, Jalan Tirta, Manukaya, Tampaksiring, Gianyar
Daily 8am–5pm

A *lingga* is a phallic symbol relating to the god Siva. In Indian Hinduism the *lingga* (also *linga* or *lingam*) is commonly revered as a symbol of Siva's generative power, but in Bali it is rarely seen. The *lingga-yoni* (literally "phallus-vagina") statue at the Tirta Empul temple is believed to be well over 1,000 years old and could be the oldest on the island.

It's hard to mistake the phallic symbolism of the *lingga*, but the *yoni* is certainly more erratic than erotic as a representation for the vagina of Shakti, goddess of fertility. Typically with a rectangular base (although sometimes curved), the *yoni* usually incorporates an extended channel at the front. This "spout" is known as a *cerat* and it is used to discharge the holy water that is poured over the top of the *lingga* by worshippers.

This is far more than simply a symbol of Siva, however. Since a central tenet of Balinese Hinduism is the balance of all things, so the paired symbols of the *lingga* and the *yoni* also stand for duality and equilibrium. Despite its rarity in Bali, the *lingga* is an extremely powerful emblem; even the cremation towers of kings were often surmounted by one. In *Secrets of Bali: Fresh Light on the Morning of the World*, authors Jonathan Copeland and Ni Wayan Murni suggest that the front wing-like vertical appendage on a ceremonial *udeng* headdress "is also a symbol for the male *lingga*" and therefore is itself symbolic of Siva.

While Tirta Empul is visited by many tourists, very few even cast a glance at the ancient *lingga-yoni* statue as they file past to the spectacularly bubbling thermal springs that have made the site a place of pilgrimage since time immemorial. On holy days, thousands of bathers queue up for purification under the cascading water in the rows of ceremonial baths. It is believed that this site was already ancient when, according to inscriptions, King Candrabhayasingha Warmadewa restored the holy bathing place – then known as "Air Mpul" – in 962 AD. While the *lingga-yoni* is overlooked by most visitors (foreigners and Balinese alike), it still receives regular offerings.

The first mention of a *lingga* in religious texts dates back to the Mahabharata, the Hindu epic written around 1500 BC, which remains one of the longest poems ever written (it comprises about 100,000 verses). As with much religious symbolism, however, the *lingga-yoni* emblem (whether in Bali or in India) has long since transcended its original representation; to Hindu worshippers it is no more an image of sexuality than a cross is a method of execution to Christians.

SACRED WHITE COWS OF TARO

20

Albino cows with mystical healing powers

Taro, Tegallalang, Gianyar
0819 3880 4562
Daily 8am–5pm

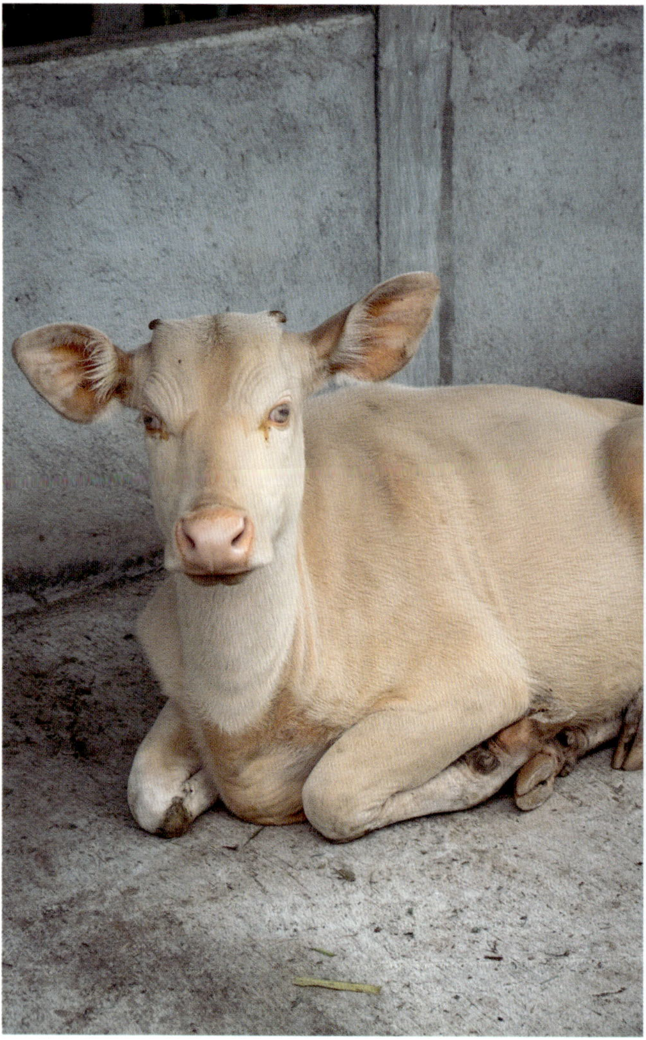

If a white cow was born in this area, the locals would be so afraid of the responsibility for raising it that they would bring it to us," says Wayan Jati, who cares for what are often described as the sacred "albino cattle" of Taro village.

According to locals, these cattle – technically not albinos but actually a unique variation of Bali cattle – are never found anywhere else on the island. "In fact, there are only 42 left in the world and they are all here in this reserve," says Wayan proudly. "They cannot survive in another area and would die if removed."

Bali is home to what might be the world's prettiest cows, the domestic offspring of Indonesia's wild *banteng* cattle. The white animals that are only found in Taro village are similar in appearance to the typical Balinese bovines – apart from the fact that their hide is a pale, creamy white all over. Such a tiny population would never be a viable gene pool, so normal bulls and cows are crossed with the white animals. Along with the ghostly pale cows in the livestock sheds there are what are listed as "black bulls" (normal Balinese bulls, far darker than the females) and "red females" (the standard tan-coloured Bali cows).

"When a white cow mates with a normal bull, the chances are about 66 per cent that the baby will be white," says Wayan, "and only the *lembu* – as the white animals are known – are sacred."

The reason these white cattle might be considered sacred can probably be traced back to the fact that a white bull is the chosen mount of the god Siva. Some people in Taro village also claim that the great Indian sage Rsi Markandeya imported white Indian cattle when he brought his teachings to the village in the 8th century. Two huge stone sculptures of cows outside the main gates of the temple dedicated to the sage in Taro village bear testimony to the continuing sanctity of these animals: while the other statues are covered in the moss you would expect from their antiquity, the cows' eyes, ears and mouths appear to have been cleaned by devotees.

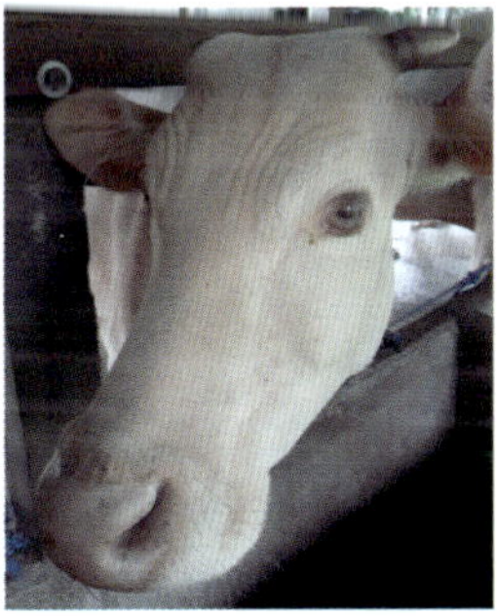

How to cure bad eyes and bad hearing

"The saliva and the urine and faeces of these animals are collected during religious processions," explains Wayan Jati, who looks after the sacred cows of Taro. "They are sacred and have medicinal properties: the tears from the eyes can cure bad eyes, for example, and even the dirt from the cows' ears can cure bad hearing. The milk, of course, is the most sacred thing of all."

PURA AGUNG GUNUNG RAUNG

21

The home of Bali's Hindu founder

Jalan Raya Taro, Tegallalang, Gianyar
Foreigners need permission from village elders to enter the temple, and must wear a sarong and sash. There is an office at the temple's northern gate; ask here for permission to enter

Each week, thousands of tourists head up to the cool mountainside village of Taro, where they visit a popular elephant safari park. But few, if any, are likely to realise that they're within a stone's throw of the place that was once the home of Rsi Markandeya, the Hindu sage who (Balinese legend has it) was the first person to set foot on Bali. Pura Agung Gunung Raung is the largest temple in Taro and was built on the place where Markandeya once lived.

To appreciate the intricacies and relevance of Pura Agung Gunung Raung, we need to venture back to the 8th century, when Markandeya is said to have left an area called Aga on the slopes of Mount Raung in East Java. According to oral history, Markandeya had made the journey once before, but because he hadn't performed the necessary offerings to the gods, his followers fell ill, so everyone returned to Java. Markandeya was better prepared on the second journey; he buried the five elements of metal (silver, iron, gold, bronze and copper, each of which have symbolic meaning in Hinduism) at the foot of the highest mountain on the island. The ritual performed at that burial is said to have been the first Hindu ceremony on Bali. Standing at that site, on the slopes of Mount Agung, is now Besakih, Bali's "Mother Temple".

With the gods placated, Markandeya's followers, thought to be the ancestors of today's Bali Aga people, settled in various places on the island. Markandeya himself decided to live in a forest clearing at the site of what is now the Pura Agung Gunung Raung temple in Taro. Unlike most temples on Bali, it does not face Mount Agung; instead, it is aligned with Mount Raung.

If you get permission to enter the temple, look out for the large *kulkul*. Villagers will tell you that once upon a time an enormous tree grew in Java. When it fell its trunk formed the bridge that animals used to cross from Java to Bali. One of the tree's flowers fell in Taro and the temple's 3-metre-long *kulkul*, villagers say, is the stem of that flower.

In the outer part of the temple, look out also for the *titi gonggang*, a rectangular hole with a bamboo "bridge" on top (shown, left), which is said to signify the border between life and death. It is a symbol that is particular to Markandeya's followers. There are also *titi gonggang* at other temples in Taro. When there has been conflict between two villagers, a ritual will be held at the *titi gonggang* to settle the dispute.

Markandeya's impact on Bali can still be felt today, it is believed that he introduced the Subak system (see page 73) – and that Pulun Mascetl, found inside Gunung Raung temple, was Bali's first Subak temple – as well as Bali's unique social and civic structures.

I WAYAN GAMA PAINTING SCHOOL

22

Detailed art produced in miniature that depicts traditional life in Bali

Jalan Raya Keliki, Keliki, Tegallalang, Ginayar
0815 5800 9878
Instagram: @nanoeari_art
Daily 8am–5pm

If your eyesight's not that great, you might want to take along your specs (and possibly a magnifying glass) when you visit I Wayan Gama Painting School in Keliki. It's here that children from the village are taught the very intricate style of art for which Keliki has become known: drawn

and painted onto sheets of paper are tiny and incredibly intricate scenes of life in Bali, as well as religious scenes and landscapes that beautifully depict the island.

"Our Keliki style is unique; it is very intricate, and it is very miniature," explains I Wayan Gama, who established the school in his home in 2005. "It can take many, many months to complete one painting, and to paint in Keliki style you need a lot of expression, time and also good eyes."

The school is open to foreigners who want to take a painting class, but its main function is to provide a space for the children of the village to learn and practise their "traditional" art. The Keliki style is said to have originated in the 1970s, started by a farmer named I Ketut Sana, one of whose teachers was I Gusti Nyoman Lempad (see page 184). It is characterised by miniature scenes and intricate details. Wayan explains that as artists age, their eyes are no longer good enough to paint in such detail. "Seldom can people who are older than 40 or 45 create art like this," he says.

Prior to 2002, almost 60 per cent of adults in Keliki were creating miniature paintings that were sold to tourists, but the bomb blast in Kuta in October 2002 resulted in a major slump in visitor numbers to the island, so most of Keliki's artists turned to farming to sustain their families. "The art of miniature painting was on the verge of being lost, and so I established this school to create a new generation of artists," says Wayan.

While it is open throughout the day and has a wide collection of art on display, the best time to visit the I Wayan Gama Painting School is over the weekends or in the afternoons, as that's when the children usually gather to practise their art. It's fascinating to watch the focus and precision with which the kids, many younger than 10 years old, work.

The children do not pay to attend the art school; they go whenever it suits them and stay as long as they want. While the children genuinely seem to enjoy creating their art, there is the added incentive of earning an income from the sale of any of their paintings; 10 per cent goes towards buying supplies for the school, and the students take the rest home to their parents, where the money is usually put towards their education. Wayan points out that most of the students tend to be the boys of the village; the girls have less spare time as they practise Balinese dance and also help with preparing food in their homes.

When they are still learning the Keliki style, the children copy the works of their teachers. As they progress they have the freedom, and confidence, to paint their own creations, some of which can take almost a year to complete. "In this village we have so much talent," says Wayan proudly, showing intricate paintings created by a boy of just nine years old.

ANGSERI HOT SPRING

23

Pretty pools with healing properties in the heart of a sacred bamboo forest

Air Panas Angseri, Angseri, Tabanan
Daily 9am–6pm

Tucked against the fringe of a sacred bamboo forest near the foot of Bukit Adeng, between verdant Bedugul and the iconic rice terraces of Jatiluwih, you'll find the hot spring of Angseri. It's a place not often visited by travellers and yet it's a particularly lovely spot to relax and unwind after a morning spent walking through the paddies of Jatiluwih, which are listed by Unesco as a cultural landscape.

The baths at the hot spring are run by the local community and are very well maintained. It's a pleasant five-minute walk from the ticket booth along a concrete path; you might see macaque monkeys in the bamboo forest adjacent to the path ("They're not like the ones in Ubud – these monkeys aren't naughty," one villager laughed), or a monitor lizard scuttling through the shrubs on the other. You'll walk accompanied by the sound of water gently running through a small irrigation channel; it's a calming journey down to a very peaceful space.

Down at the spring, the water is channelled into different bathing areas. In the hottest pool, which is next to a small (cold water) waterfall, the temperature is usually around 45 degrees Celcius. The water there is a murky emerald green – excellent for easing rheumatism, the people of Angseri say. There are also nine private "pool rooms", similar to a sauna but not as steamy, which you're allowed to occupy for 30 minutes at a time. In the largest pool, the water is a "mild" 30 degrees.

Landscaping around the pools is carefully maintained and the gardens are shady and pretty. Along the path down to the spring there are a few *warungs* where meals are very reasonably priced.

To reach the location of the hot spring you'll drive through a dense bamboo forest – this forest is sacred, and despite bamboo being such a useful plant, no one is allowed to cut any of it down.

The rice terraces at nearby Jatiluwih are a part of what Unesco identifies as "Subak Landscape of Catur Angga Batukaru" and are said to be the oldest in Bali. According to Unesco, there are five sites that form part of the cultural landscape: Pura Ulun Danu Batur and Pura Taman Ayun water temples, Lake Batur, and the Pekerisan watershed near Ubud. Of these, the pretty terraces around Jatiluwih are definitely the quietest in terms of visitors.

PURA LUHUR PUCAK PETALI

24

A temple dedicated to the "God of Thieves"

Jalan Pura Petali, Jatiluwih, Penebel, Tabanan
You can view the temple from outside because, unless there is a ceremony, the gates are padlocked

A pretty drive past the Unesco-accredited rice paddies of Jatiluwih brings you to a potholed road that finally peters out at what must be one of Bali's most mysterious temples. Part of the forest opposite the temple has been fenced off to incarcerate a small herd of Timor deer and a few barking deer, but you're unlikely to see any other signs of life.

Pura Luhur Pucak Petali is dedicated to Sang Hyang Maling (the God of Thieves), and it is said that this is the place to pray if you want to become adept at the thieving trade. There is one other such temple on the island (Pura Besikalung, about 3 km away), yet it is a mystery why these temples were built or by whom.

In their excellent book *Secrets of Bali: Fresh Light on the Morning of the World*, Jonathan Copeland and Ni Wayan Murni quote a local scholar who told them that the Balinese have "the concept of a 'social bandit', a Robin Hood character, and the God of Thieves represents this ideal." It seems that there are few cultures in the world where the benevolent bandit – stealing from the rich to give to the poor – is not celebrated; history is punctuated with the names of bandit "heroes": Dick Turpin, Pancho Villa, Billy the Kid, Ned Kelly. Nor is this merely an historic phenomenon: Phoolan Devi, known as the "Bandit Queen", became so popular that she was a member of the Indian parliament when she was shot and killed (at the age of 38) in 2001.

The jungle-clad slopes of Batukaru Mountain could have been an ideal hideout for bandit gangs. In 1605 the king of Buleleng sent a force into this area, but they were chased away by a swarm of millions of bees when (for unknown reasons) they attacked the 11th century Batukaru Temple.

Guesswork aside, the reason for the existence of a temple dedicated to the God of Thieves remains unknown. In 2002 *The Jakarta Post* reported that there had not been a resident priest at Pura Petali for many years, and that Sang Hyang Maling had strict requirements for thieves who were asking his blessing, stipulating that they should "only steal moderately". A priest from a nearby temple told the reporter, "The thieves should only steal things when necessary and shouldn't use the stolen goods extravagantly."

Theoretically, it is still possible for thieves to visit this spot to ask for blessings; there are usually offerings at the shrines near the little parking area. "People here are no longer interested in becoming social bandits," the priest explained. "People only come to the temple to ask for holy water for the protection of their belongings."

Perhaps there's a certain logic in asking the God of Thieves for protection from his own devotees.

MARGARANA NATIONAL MONUMENT PARK

25

Spiritual resting place of Bali's freedom fighters

Marga Dauh Puri, Marga, Tabanan
Daily 8am–5pm

Normandy, Rorke's Drift, Wounded Knee – the resting places of fallen warriors are invariably powerful and spiritual. Set in pretty countryside, just at the point where the rice paddies begin to merge with the lower slopes of Batukaru Mountain, Bali's Margarana National Monument Park is no exception.

The graves – most marked with a Hindu swastika – are purely symbolic, since most warriors would have been cremated, and the few Muslims would have been buried on the day of their death.

The 10-metre-long marble plaque on the wall outside the complex shows the names and hometowns of 1,372 independence fighters who were killed between 1945 and 1950 in what became known as the Indonesian National Revolution. While Indonesia declared *kemerdekaan* (independence) in 1945 – two days after the surrender of the Japanese emperor and removal of the occupying forces – it wasn't until 1949 that the Netherlands recognised it as a free state.

By the end of World War II the Dutch had been weakened by German occupation, and without a loan of US$10 million from the American government (equal to about US$140 million today) to finance a restoration of Dutch control in Indonesia, it is doubtful if they could have returned to their Far Eastern colony. The result was more than four years of guerrilla warfare. The neatly maintained ranks of grave markers near the village of Marga bear testimony to the brutality of those years. This location was the scene of a ritual *puputan* (fight to the death) led by Independence hero I Gusti Ngurah Rai (see page 66), whose name may be familiar even to the newest arrivals at Bali's international airport, and whose portrait is on the Rp50,000 note. On 20 November 1946, 29-year-old Lieutenant Colonel Ngurah Rai led 96 Indonesian soldiers in the desperate fight that came to be known as the Margarana (Battle of Marga) against Dutch forces, who were backed up by air strikes.

By 1947 Dutch operations (described officially as "police actions to restore law and order") had provoked international recriminations and even the U.S. were clearly wishing they hadn't been so generous in funding such bloodshed. It is said that 2,300 Dutch soldiers died between 1945 and 1949, but some estimates say that Indonesian fatalities may have run to more than 100,000.

While the Margarana memorial site is a place of homage for Indonesian armed forces and the site of a parade on 20 November each year, you're unlikely to see many visitors here. On a bright sunlit Balinese morning it can be very hard to imagine this beautiful hillside as a battlefield.

It was only as late as 2005 that the Netherlands officially accepted 1949 as the year of independence for the Republic of Indonesia.

BALI BUTTERFLY PARK

26

Moths and butterflies from around Indonesia

Jalan Batukaru, Sesandan, Tabanan
Daily 8am–5pm
Entry: Rp85,000 per adult; Rp45,000 per child

As the land starts to rise from Tabanan towards the slopes of Batukaru (a dormant volcano and the second highest peak on Bali), so the air begins to cool. The climate becomes wetter, the vegetation a little more lush – the perfect habitat for butterflies.

It's for this very reason that the Bali Butterfly Park was established in the village of Wanasari. The park was started in 1993 by six lepidopterologists (butterfly enthusiasts) who wanted to create a place that would both conserve butterflies and educate people about these pretty insects. It is now home to about 25 species of butterflies and moths from around Indonesia.

The park is a large, carefully landscaped garden protected by a shade-cloth "tent" and incorporates flowing water and lots of vegetation. "This is real butterfly habitat," says Luh Putu Sri Wahyuni, who has worked at the park since 2005. "In here are the plants that butterflies love, but there are also their predators, like praying mantis, here."

Putu spends most of her working days inside a protected space that is the nursery of the park: the place where butterflies and moths emerge from their cocoons and dry their wings. "These creatures don't have a very long lifespan," she explains. "Some of them live just a few days, while others can live up to three weeks."

To the untrained eye it can be difficult to tell the difference between a moth and a butterfly, but Putu says there are some surprisingly simple traits to look out for: butterflies tend to hold their wings up while resting, whereas moths will hold them open; if you see a caterpillar and it has tiny hairs on its body, it will become a moth.

The majestic Attacus Atlas moth – called a *borong* in Indonesian – is the star of the show in this little nursery. They are the largest species in the park (Putu recalls one specimen that had a wingspan of 30 cm), and yet they live for only five days. Take a careful look at its wings and you'll see how its colouring acts as protection from predators by mimicking the appearance of a snake.

The best time to be here is before 10am and after 3pm, as the butterflies are most active outside of the hottest hours of the day. But no matter what time you're there you're likely to be delighted by the hundreds of butterflies that flit through the garden.

> In one pavilion there are some enormous stick insects, as well as scorpions and rhinoceros beetles. Not much information is available on these insects, but it's a good photo opportunity if you don't mind the insects climbing on you.

BALI WILDLIFE RESCUE CENTRE ㉗

A chance to see (and help) Indonesia's unique wildlife

Jalan Teratai no. 49, Dauh Peken, Tabanan
0361 894 1677
fnpf.org
Daily 9am–4pm

Bali Wildlife Rescue Centre has facilities to offer shelter to almost 100 birds and animals, and you are likely to see as many as 30 different species here at any one time. This is an animal hospital and rehabilitation centre where a mind-boggling variety of creatures can be prepared for release back into the wild.

The centre has five full-time staff members (including experienced veterinarians) and counts on the support of volunteers, who arrange their visits through local hotels in Tabanan or via Airbnb Experiences. You will see the critically endangered Bali starling and the protected black-winged starling, as well as kites, parrots, hornbills, eagles and various birds-of-paradise that are waiting for return to their natural habitat. Many of these creatures have been confiscated from smugglers and collectors, or from the Satria Bird Market (see page 32) in Denpasar. They are quarantined on arrival then caged in conditions that are as natural as possible to try to prepare them for the wild.

Some of these creatures are so injured or traumatised (or have been captive for so long) that they can never be released – the centre can only attempt to give them a comfortable home for the rest of their lives. There is a sun bear that will be returned to Sumatra when funds and papers are accumulated (it had been waiting for 18 months when we visited), and a pair of binturong "bear cats", which you will learn are neither bears nor cats but actually oversized palm civets. Even more "over-sized" are the giant crocodiles; it turns out that these are the mysterious "man-eating escapees" from the crocodile ponds at the abandoned Taman Festival theme park (see page 12).

The centre receives funding in the form of donations from (occasional) visitors and volunteers, and is supported by Friends of the National Parks Foundation. The costs of trans-location and the bureaucracy involved in transporting protected species to their natural habitats in Kalimantan, Sumatra or West Papua means that some inmates stay at Bali Wildlife Rescue Centre much longer than anticipated. Some of the creatures you are likely to see are crowned pigeons, yellow-crested cockatoos, variegated hornbills, civets (often rescued from confinement in atrocious *kopi luwak* establishments), green tree pythons, southern pig-tailed macaques and ebony leaf monkeys. Known locally simply as *monyet hitam* (black monkeys), these gibbon-like primates are often sought after for ceremonial sacrifices.

THE OGOH-OGOH BALI MUSEUM ㉘

A haunting reunion of some of Bali's most outrageous demons

Jalan Ayodya, Mengwi, Badung
0821 4622 1180
theogohogohbali.business.site
Daily 9am–6pm

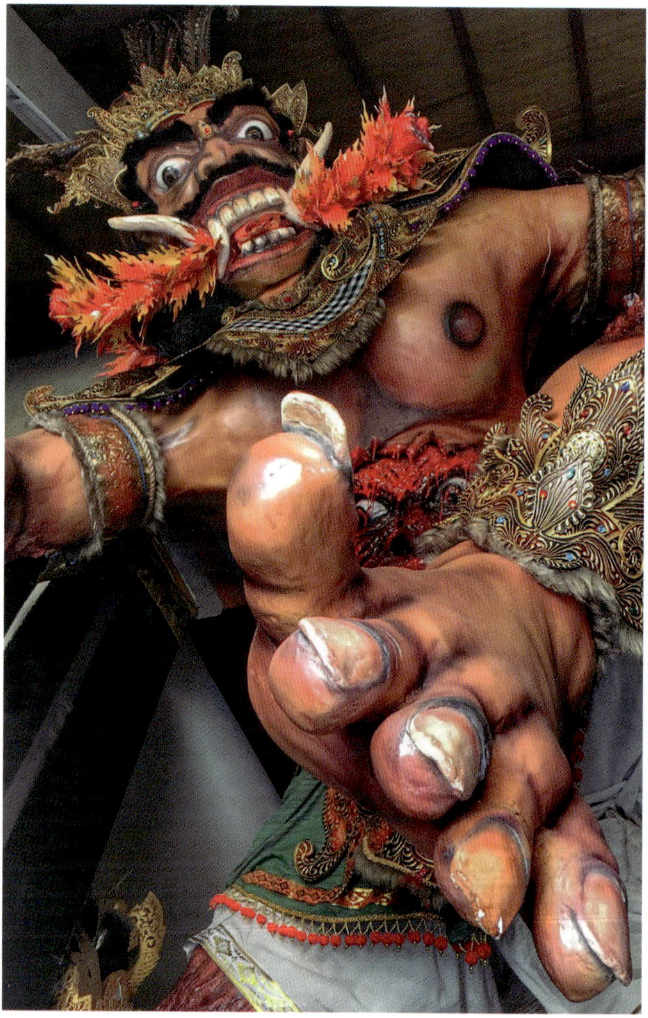

It's an unnerving feeling to walk into what seems to be an abandoned barn and find yourself dwarfed by leering and snarling demons. Few people ever visit this exhibition of some of the most dramatic Ogoh-Ogoh ever collected together in one place. (Even the attendant might not be there, so just slip your admission fee in the box by the door).

This collection of 38 hellish effigies – many looming over 6 metres tall – were originally constructed as a sort of "party invitation" for the most diabolical demons of the Hindu epic *Ramayana*. The purification ceremony known as Ngrupuk, which takes place on the eve of Nyepi (the Balinese "Day of Silence", see page 24), is carried out amidst a cacophony of noise, lights and flame. Bouncing, gyrating Ogoh-Ogoh are carried through every village in Bali on the shoulders of local men. By midnight the Ogoh-Ogoh are destroyed (traditionally burned on the beach or at the cemetery) and the Balinese (along with everyone else) hurry inside their houses for the day of silence (which lasts until daylight on the second day). During the day of silence there can be no smoke from cooking fires, lights from houses or even loud talking; transport is totally halted on all the island's roads, and even the airspace over Bali is closed. The silence fools the demons into thinking that nobody lives on the island after all. Disappointed, they return to their dominions and leave Bali alone for another year.

Occasionally the best of the Ogoh-Ogoh survive their fate, and some make it here to this spectacular little museum. Technically, the constructions (made of wood, bamboo, papier-mâché and polystyrene) are impressive; emphasis is placed on Ogoh-Ogoh that seem to balance precariously from the smallest point of support, so that they appear to dance when they're carried. The name Ogoh-Ogoh comes from a Balinese term for something that is shaken, but even in a static pose the museum's collection is a spectacularly frenetic jumble of snarling beasts.

Mostly they were built by various village youth organisations known as Sekaa Truna Truni; while the imagery is frequently directed at famous warriors from Hindu mythology, there also seems to be a lot of focus placed on pendulous demonic breasts of every shape imaginable.

SANGEH MONKEY FOREST

(29)

Bali's "other" monkey forest

Obyek Wisata Sangeh, Jalan Brahmana, Sangeh, Badung
bukit-sari-sangeh.com
Daily 7:30am–6pm

The village of Sangeh boasts a 14-hectare forest of 2,000 towering nutmeg trees – home now to troupes of curious macaque monkeys – that were planted in the 17th century to form part of the royal garden of the Mengwi kingdom. It's cool and often breezy in the forest, offering welcome respite from Bali's tropical heat, yet relatively few outsiders seem to know about it.

Between the trees, which stand almost 45 metres straight up, a network of paths links four temples. Pura Bukit Sari is the main temple here; it has a nine-level meru tower dedicated to the Hindu god Vishnu. While it is still a very sacred place, the ornate gateway now forms the backdrop for many pre-wedding photography sessions. If you come across one of these shoots you're in luck; you will have the chance to see the spectacular traditional wedding attire.

There are hundreds of macaque monkeys living in three troupes within the sacred forest at Sangeh. They're less intimidating than their cousins up the road in Ubud but it's still best not to get too close. What's curious here is this: sometimes a monkey from this forest will "adopt" a kitten from the village and literally love it to death. It's not unusual, the temple guards say, to see a monkey holding onto a tiny kitten, grooming it and clenching it to their body as the monkey leaps from tree to tree. Eventually the kittens die, however, because the monkeys can't give them the nutrition they need to survive.

The Ubud Monkey Forest is said to be the most popular tourist spot on the island – thousands of visitors enter this sacred place every month, wandering the shaded pathways that are the domain of the rather brazen monkeys. With moss-covered carvings and plants that grow over walls and bridges, it certainly can be an evocative place if you're there when it's quiet ... but Sangeh Monkey Forest, just a 10-minute drive away, is even more intriguing and far removed from the Ubud crowds.

Did you know ...

The nutmeg trees (*Dipterocarpus trinervis*) that grow at Sangeh are not of the same species that is native to the Maluku Islands in north-eastern Indonesia, which produce edible nutmeg seeds. That species (*Myristica fragrans*) was highly sought after during the spice trade days, and it was because of the nutmeg, mace and cloves found on these islands that they became known as the Spice Islands.

TAMAN MUMBUL SANGEH 30

A beautifully serene place for a magical legend

Tirta Taman Mumbul Sangeh, off Jalan Raya Sangeh, Sangeh, Badung
Daily 6am–7pm
Free entry, donations welcome

Once upon a time in central Bali – so the legend goes – there was an old woman who would walk from village to village carrying a large jug of water. She would sell the water to those who needed it; it was how she earned a living. One afternoon in the dry season, the old woman reached the village of Sangeh. Exhausted from the intense heat along her journey, she sat under a tree to rest. As she looked around she noticed that even under the shade of the trees, the plants were also affected by the heat. They were limp and wilting; some were dying. The old woman took pity on them and poured water from her jug over the parched vegetation. At first she watered the plants beside her, and when the water continued to flow she nourished the plants a little further way, and further still. The water didn't stop flowing, and eventually formed the small lake that you can visit today, just outside the village of Sangeh.

A statue of the old woman and her water jug stands at the base of a banyan tree on the edge of the aquamarine lake. It's a beautifully serene place that's surrounded by trees – a magical setting, watched over by the water temple just below the lake.

There are a few water temples around Ubud that (probably thanks to Instagram and evocative images of people praying under falling water) have become popular spots for tourists. Tirta Taman Mumbul in Sangeh, however, remains delightfully off the radar.

How to be cleansed of negative energy

The water enters the lake from a spring and flows into Tirta Taman Mumbul, the water temple (*tirta* means "holy water"), via 11 ducts built below 11 Hindu deities. If you chose to enter this water temple you need to wear a sarong, and as you wade through the pool and pass under the falling water, Hindu belief says, you are cleansed of negative energy.

The lake's water performs another important function: it flows into crafted channels and sustains local agriculture, forming a part of the area's Subak system. The Subak (see page 73) – recognised by Unesco as part of the Cultural Heritage of Bali – is a centuries-old cooperative social system that reflects the Balinese philosophy of Tri Hita Karana: harmony among people, nature and the environment. The success of rice farming in Bali (see page 48) is usually attributed to the management of water resources through the Subak.

BEDUGAL TAMAN REKREASI RESORT

31

Welcome to Bali's "Ghost Palace Hotel"

Jalan Baturiti Bedugul, Bedugul, Tabanan
There is a chain across the entrance; ask at the neighbouring warung for permission to enter

As the road twists and turns south from Lake Beratan in Bali's highlands it offers wonderful views over shallow valleys of strawberry fields and vegetable crops down towards the flatlands of Bali. It's tempting to keep your eye on the panorama, but about a kilometre below the edge of the lake, look "inland" to the left just after you make a tight hairpin bend and you'll see the entrance to Bedugal Taman Rekreasi Resort. On an overcast or rainy day the short, steep driveway creates a particularly eerie entry to what many people call "Ghost Palace Hotel".

The Bedugal Taman Rekreasi Resort is abandoned; it has been since 1998, only six months after its grand opening. There are many theories behind why the hotel closed and has never reopened, ranging from murder charges and corrupt politicians to bankruptcy and disagreements between investors. One tale even goes that one night, every single guest in the new 140-room hotel simply vanished and the hotel has been empty and haunted ever since.

"It's not haunted," laughs Pak Made, who worked as a cleaner at the hotel while it was open and who now has a small *warung* right next to its entrance. "Yes, there are stories of ghosts, but I've never seen one."

When you explore the abandoned hotel it's hard to brush ghost stories aside, however. Across five acres the hotel wraps around the mountainside; the sturdy buildings stand strong but are being strangled and reclaimed by nature. Wander through the vast, empty halls and rooms and you'll see creepers tangling their way over staircases, shallow puddles reflecting corridors of pillars, green algae creeping its way across glass picture windows. Black algae thrives and gives an aged, haunted look to the statues in the overgrown gardens, while mosses and ferns have colonised gaps in the concrete of vast courtyards.

The hotel grounds provide so many opportunities for photographers. Take a torch if you'd like to explore deep in the buildings, but be aware that the floors can be slippery, especially in the damper sections of the buildings.

It's not unusual when you drive around Bali to see potential hotel buildings that have been abandoned before completion. Even so, there are more than 5,500 hotels on the island – that's about one every square kilometre – with many more on the drawing board and under construction.

TAMAN USADA

32

A garden to cure (almost) all ailments

Bali Botanic Garden, Jalan Kebun Raya, Candikuning, Tabanan
0368 203 3211
balibotanicgarden.org
Daily 8am–6pm

Traditional medicine *(usada)* has always been an integral part of life in Bali. Still today if you mention an ailment while in any village on the island, someone is likely to offer advice on what plant could help to alleviate the symptoms. Of course, it's the *balian* – traditional healers – who have a wealth of knowledge of traditional medicine, much of which has been passed down through the ages via lontar manuscripts (see page 161).

In the cool, misty hills of Bedugul, the 157-hectare Bali Botanic Garden is the largest botanic garden in Indonesia. In a quiet corner of this garden, almost a kilometre from the entrance gate, is Taman Usada. This small section of the property has been set aside for growing, documenting, researching and preserving some of the most valuable plants on the island – those used in traditional medicine. Of the almost 500 species of medicinal plants mentioned in the lontar manuscripts, more than 300 species, including 15 very rare ones, are grown in the 1.6-hectare Taman Usada.

The information available around the garden is sparse but interesting. Jasmine flowers, for example, the national flower of Indonesia, can be used to treat the common cold, diarrhoea and toothache. Betel leaves, a wonderful antiseptic, used to be combined with lime and used in Java to remove arsenic from the blades of *kerises* (see page 196).

While this quiet pocket within the botanic garden will appeal to those with an interest in health and botany, the garden as a whole is well worth a visit. The trees of the tropical forest are enormous, and the property is said to have the largest collection of wild orchids in Bali, as well as the world's most comprehensive begonia collection. It is extremely picturesque, and a wander through the 200 species of ferns and mosses in the fern garden is a real step back in time.

Jamu is a traditional medicine that is made from a variety of roots, leaves, bark and flowers. There are literally thousands of recipes for *jamu* that will treat a wide assortment of ailments. The origin of *jamu* is said to be Central Java, but these days it is found all over Bali. If you're near a fruit market in the early mornings, you're very likely to see *mbok jamu* – a woman carrying a basket of *jamu* bottles that could treat everything from a bad stomach to menstrual pains, increase a woman's beauty or a man's strength. The basic ingredients of *jamu* are usually turmeric and ginger, with honey added for sweetness. The village of Penglipuran (see page 204) is known for *loloh cemcem*, a green *jamu* made from *cemcem* leaves (or hog plum, *Spondias pinnata*), young coconut water and palm sugar.

It was September 1995 and Thomas Jonglez was in Peshawar, the northern Pakistani city 20 kilometres from the tribal zone he was to visit a few days later. It occurred to him that he should record the hidden aspects of his native city, Paris, which he knew so well. During his seven-month trip back home from Beijing, the countries he crossed included Tibet (entering clandestinely, hidden under blankets in an overnight bus), Iran and Kurdistan. He never took a plane but travelled by boat, train or bus, hitchhiking, cycling, on horseback or on foot, reaching Paris just in time to celebrate Christmas with the family.

On his return, he spent two fantastic years wandering the streets of the capital to gather material for his first "secret guide", written with a friend. For the next seven years he worked in the steel industry until the passion for discovery overtook him. He launched Jonglez Publishing in 2003 and moved to Venice three years later.

In 2013, in search of new adventures, the family left Venice and spent six months travelling to Brazil via North Korea, Micronesia, the Solomon Islands, Easter Island, Peru and Bolivia.

After seven years in Rio de Janeiro, he now lives in Berlin with his wife and three children.

Jonglez Publishing produces a range of titles in nine languages, released in 40 countries.

ATLASES

Atlas of extreme weather
Atlas of forbidden places
Atlas of geographical curiosities
Atlas of unusual wines

PHOTO BOOKS

Abandoned America
Abandoned Asylums
Abandoned Australia
Abandoned Belgium
Abandoned Churches: Unclaimed places of worship
Abandoned cinemas of the world
Abandoned France
Abandoned Germany
Abandoned Italy
Abandoned Japan
Abandoned Lebanon
Abandoned Spain
Abandoned USSR
Abandoned world – An AI-generated exploration
After the Final Curtain – The Fall of the American Movie Theater
After the Final Curtain – America's Abandoned Theaters
Baikonur – Vestiges of the Soviet space programme
Cinemas – A French heritage
Clickbait – A visual journey through AI-generated stories
Forbidden France
Forbidden Places – Vol. 1
Forbidden Places – Vol. 2
Forbidden Places – Vol. 3
Forgotten France
Forgotten Heritage
Oblivion
Secret sacred sites
Venice deserted
Venice from the skies

'SOUL OF' GUIDES

Soul of Amsterdam
Soul of Athens
Soul of Barcelona
Soul of Berlin
Soul of Brussels
Soul of Detroit
Soul of Kyoto
Soul of Lisbon
Soul of Los Angeles
Soul of Marrakesh
Soul of Marseille
Soul of Milan
Soul of New York
Soul of Paris
Soul of Rome
Soul of Tokyo
Soul of Venice
Soul of Vienna

'SECRET' GUIDES

Secret Amsterdam
Secret Bangkok
Secret Barcelona
Secret Bath – An unusual guide
Secret Belfast
Secret Berlin
Secret Boston – An unusual guide
Secret Brighton – An unusual guide
Secret Brooklyn
Secret Brussels
Secret Budapest
Secret Buenos Aires
Secret Campania
Secret Cape Town
Secret Copenhagen
Secret Corsica
Secret Dolomites
Secret Dublin – An unusual guide
Secret Edinburgh – An unusual guide
Secret Florence
Secret French Riviera
Secret Geneva
Secret Glasgow
Secret Granada
Secret Helsinki
Secret Johannesburg
Secret Lisbon
Secret Liverpool – An unusual guide
Secret London – An unusual guide
Secret London – Unusual bars & restaurants
Secret Los Angeles – An unusual guide
Secret Louisiana – An unusual guide
Secret Madrid
Secret Mexico City
Secret Milan
Secret Montreal – An unusual guide
Secret Naples
Secret New Orleans
Secret New York – An unusual guide
Secret New York – Curious activities
Secret New York – Hidden bars & restaurants
Secret Normandy
Secret Paris
Secret Prague
Secret Provence
Secret Rio
Secret Rome
Secret Seville
Secret Singapore
Secret Stockholm
Secret Sussex – An unusual guide
Secret Tokyo
Secret Tuscany
Secret Vienna
Secret Venice
Secret Washington D.C.
Secret York – An unusual guide

Follow us on Facebook and Instagram

ACKNOWLEDGEMENTS

The authors would like to extend thanks to the countless Balinese people who have been so willing to share information on their history and culture, and without whom this book would not exist. An immeasurable debt of gratitude is due to our close friend Sudana and his family (Ketut, Kadek, Komang and Ayu), whose knowledge of the intricacies of Balinese tradition and culture shines through on many of these pages.

Mark's 14-year-old daughter Lucia also acted as a dedicated research assistant on some of the most exciting locations in this book.

Thanks also to Thomas Jonglez, who had the vision to produce guides that are aimed especially at readers with a fascination for some of the most intriguing places on our planet. We hope that this book will inspire people to explore a little more widely into what might still be – even now – the world's most beautiful island.

PHOTOGRAPHY CREDITS

All photos by **Narina Exelby** and **Mark Eveleigh,** except:
Mekar Bhuana: © Mekar Bhuana Centre

Cartography: Louisa Keyworth – **Design:** Emmanuelle Willard Toulemonde – **Editing:** Matt Gay – **Proofreading:** Eleni Salemi – **Publishing:** Clémence Mathé

Registration of copyright: May 2025 – Edition: 02

ISBN: 978-2-36195-898-5

Printed in Bulgaria by Dedrax